PRAISE FOR JUSTIN MARLOWE

Justin Marlowe's keen observations and emotional honesty make this memoir a compelling read. The reader is left with a profound sense of empathy for Marlowe's journey, eager to follow his path through the complexities of adolescence. Marlowe's writing is a reminder that even in moments of uncertainty and heartache, there is a strength and resilience that carries us forward.

— CLAY DOUG, WORLD POETRY
COLLECTIVE

PERFECT STRANGERS

PERFECT STRANGERS

Echoes of a
Black Suburban Youth

JUSTIN
MARLOWE

EMPOWERED
PRESS

Published in the United States by the Empowered Press Las Cruces, NM

ISBN: 978-1-957430-22-5 (paperback)

ISBN: 978-1-957430-23-2 (ebook)

Library of Congress Cataloging-Publication-Data is available

http://theempoweredpress.com

publish@theempoweredpress.com

Cover Design: Onur Aksoy

http://onegraphica.com

The Empowered Press can bring authors to your live event. For more information or to book an event, please email: publish@theempoweredpress.com

This project is dedicated in loving memory to Terry Keith Marlowe 1956-2008 and to my mother, Valerie Marlowe, for their continuous love and support.

Disclaimer:
Nothing that I have or will say in this piece is designed to paint my parents, or anyone, in a pejorative light. Everything that I convey is simply based on my views and experiences, from my vantage point.

———

Analyze your situation, and then speak your truth. Become revolutionary. Be extreme. Be bold. Be fearless. Continue to explore your curiosities about the world we live in. You can admonish the individuals who make up a revolution, but you cannot reprimand the psyche of the people. Let your mind, words, and actions advocate for continued progression, no matter what obstacles may stand in your way. Let them perceive you for your worth and what you embody. Fight against the metaphorical machines that have aligned themselves with the intent to counteract your evolution.

———

PHASE 1

1

The terms "perfect" and "strange" are typically used in a mutually exclusive manner. No connection or resemblance to one another with regards to conventional custom. "Perfect" is loosely defined as "having all the required or desirable elements, qualities, or characteristics; as good as it is possible to be." On the other hand, "strange" would imply something "unusual or surprising in a way that is unsettling or hard to understand." Now, this doesn't innately mean that pairing the two expressions together would be unsuitable. And it's that which makes their usage in tandem so intriguing. This is my story up until the end of the eleventh grade, but it's best told in conjunction with my best friend, Nicos. Two societal outliers who merged together within life's random conditions, almost like scripted performance art. My tale is particularly nuanced, which is why intricate background information surrounding Nicos is integral to the overall understanding of the story as a coming-of-age piece. Furthermore, this prompts me to start with myself.

I, Justin Alexander Marlowe, am a conglomerate of a multitude of elements, many of which seem to be extremely contradictory if you're the type to pay close attention to general stereotypes. I was born on April 20, 1983, in the nation's capital and political center, Washington, DC, at the Walter Reed National Military Medical Center. I'm a 4/20 baby. As I got older, this particular date would become the subject of many facetiously sly grins whenever my driver's license was shown. I'm the oldest of three siblings, which includes my younger brother, Jonathan, and sister, Shayna, who is the youngest of us all. I'm the offspring of my father, Terry, who was a dedicated officer in the United States Army for more than twenty years, and mother, Valerie, who was a devout kindergarten teacher for more than thirty years. Both were born in the mid-1950s, with my father being from Nuremberg, Germany (his parents were stationed there for a brief period) and my mother from Wilmington, Delaware—products of an emerging Black middle class.

Terry was the first in his family to attend college. That notion may not seem like a significant accomplishment in a modern sense, but at the time it was considered remarkable. As a young man, my dad was a real standout amongst many of his peers as both an athlete and a student. He ended up using the army as a vehicle to obtain a business degree. During her early years, my mother moved from rural Delaware to Washington, DC, where opportunities for Blacks were more plentiful.

My parents could always provide most of our desired amenities to us as children, no matter how unnecessary they really were. We lived in a pretty loving home. It would have seemed fairly standard to an outsider. No *glaring* elements of trauma or anything off-kilter. As a family, we reaped the benefits of having a military parent as well as one who taught children for a living. They were both exceptional people at their core, but nuances go a long way in shaping a persona. We traveled all over the United States and even spent a two-year stint in Stuttgart, Germany, which led to most of my earliest developmental memories. My family moved there in 1988 when I was about five years old. It contributed to all sorts of jaunts across Western Europe in our little brown Mitsubishi minivan.

Trips to Paris, Italy, Switzerland, Austria, Turkey, Spain, and

Poland (the countries I can recall off the top of my head). I was visiting castles, concentration camps, restaurants, major cities, arcades, etc. Nothing really seemed off-limits. I guess one could say it was a total mindfuck in the sense of giving a five-year-old a bit of a haughty mental disposition. Feelings of privilege were definitely ingrained in me from an early age, and very little adversity was experienced at that time. Needless to say, being Black with this disposition wasn't exactly "run of the mill" as I've come to understand it as an adult. However, I didn't know anything different at the age of five.

German customs are a bit dissimilar from American ones, which was to be expected. They are quite particular about punctuality. Do not be early, and definitely do not be late (unfortunately, this didn't stick with me). I also remember them being adamant about shaking hands as a form of greeting, even as a kid. More so than we do here in the States. I recall the streets of Stuttgart looking like something out of a George Lucas film. Always so freshly swept. No degenerate types in the alleys. Never any overflowing trash on street corners or outside of restaurants. Such pristine playgrounds and common areas. The high rises gave an appearance similar to that of the fictitious Delta City from the first *RoboCop*. There was a delicatessen across the street from our apartment, which led to the early morning scent of freshly cut bologna. I don't even know why I remember this, but it always stood out to me. It's the primary reason why I love bologna so much today. In the United States, bologna is considered one of the lower-class meats, but it was very different in Germany. Whenever I buy it now, I feel like I'm saving money. I could be wrong regarding my perceptions, but these are just observations from the past.

The school I attended, Boeblingen Elementary, looked absolutely untouched. Floors were particularly glistening and slick. It easily had the cleanest appearance I would ever experience outside of institutions of higher learning. So much attention was paid to the details that Americans might take for granted.

Maybe it's because it was a Department of Defense school. Increased funding for education can do wonders. They even had a mandatory foreign language program, which required all of its students to learn German, starting with the kindergarteners— such a great age to institute foreign language requirements. The mind is a sponge, especially during those years. I made some acquaintances and was into athletics. Nobody I bonded with would become a lifelong friend or anything, but I was social. Basketball and T-ball were my sports of choice. We even had some family stationed in Stuttgart, so having some familiar Black faces around was comforting.

2

My earliest memories of overt sexual curiosity occurred in my kindergarten classroom. Mrs. Dayhoff, my teacher, didn't seem to notice anything suspicious or strange. I suppose I was fairly covert with my behaviors. Some might call them toxic, but I was just doing what I perceived as being instinctual. If a girl ever stood on a chair or table, I'd do whatever I could to try and position myself beneath her in order to look up her dress or skirt. As early as I can remember, I had a thing for the scent of a girl or woman. I'm not exactly sure why this was the case, but I saw women as pristine beings. Like delicate little flowers, regardless of how abrasive they may have been in real life.

My father had a friend, Cameron, who occasionally visited our apartment with his girlfriend. I think her name was Kiki, but I'm not completely sure. I've always thought of Kiki as an appealing name, so maybe that's just wishful thinking on my part. She was absolutely gorgeous, with a bit of a Jody Watley–type vibe. Tall, slender, chocolate-colored skin, and always wearing form-fitting skirts. Any chance that I got to be close to her seemed like a privilege, and I was incessantly attempting to smell her hair, which was huge and always very teased and full of hairspray. A woman's aroma has endlessly stood out to me, so in those kindergarten classroom moments, part of my motive was to acquire some insight into how a young lady smelled. I didn't even think about the fact that young people don't bathe frequently. Was I acting as a typical young male or delving into something that was more indicative of future fetishes? Who really knows? Nothing ever manifested in my favor. But it was all in good fun, and I never got caught. I didn't turn into a Peeping Tom or anything.

This was just some of the stuff occurring within my world. But very few fruitful things come without drawbacks. Although we had everything we needed and were able to do lots of traveling, there was a certain amount of rigidity that came with living in a military home. Some of my very first mental efforts came with navigating these strict boundaries, mainly in terms of making sense of the why. The overall stringency was magnified by having a mother who was a teacher. Her emphasis on education was paramount to almost everything else. It sometimes appeared that she was playing the role of a teacher, even at home. With that being said, one quality of hers I must emphasize is how she always worked extremely hard at anything of significant meaning to her. This largely played into her success as an educator and even later in her life as a prodigious caretaker. She was one of those "first person in and last one to leave" type of individuals. Some find that trait to be annoying, but I think it's actually pretty admirable. Although I felt like she played the part of an educator far too often, she paid very close attention to all that involved home decor, always presented herself with an uplifting disposition, and loved extremely hard. She was also a phenomenal cook. She did such a fantastic job placing her family into a realm that presented immaculately. Positive *intentions* were consistently present.

Establishing right from wrong was usually very polar. Good vs. evil; righteous vs. the unrighteous; love vs. hate. Simple concepts, right? The hero represents nobility, and the villain encompasses elements of corruption and vileness. In other words, no gray area was open to interpretation or objective morality. Behavioral expectations were stressed. There was very little leeway, as giving the appearance of having everything "kept together" seemed to be more important than one's emotional stability. More attention was given to developing on the outside, as opposed to on the interior. It would become rather uncomfortable, especially as one was emerging with regard to their perspectives on the world around them. On one hand, you're constantly being told what and how to do things.

On the other hand, you seem to have far more freedom than the average person. Making sense of those liberties was not discussed. One's feelings and emotions were left to be dealt with in isolation. Intrinsically, you know being Black comes with some social drawbacks, yet you aren't really restricting anything you do in terms of how you live your life. Most of my Black peers (consisting only of a few classmates and one set of extended family members) in Europe seemed to be living the same way. Later in life, I would come to understand that the Black experience in the United States was nothing like it was in Europe. In the meantime, I learned about the overreaching social drawbacks that African Americans faced by osmosis in the home. Those tiny pieces of knowledge brought with them some substantial questions, but I was beginning to gain insights into society, which would become integral in terms of internalizing social viewpoints that were universally held by others. These represented a mild piece of growth, even at such a young age.

3

When you pay close attention to what the adults around you talk about, it really helps you gain perspective. Both of my parents were from the Washington, DC, area and were raised during the era of "bussing" within the public school system. If you're not familiar with the term, it's defined as "the practice of assigning and transporting students to schools within or outside their local school districts in an effort to diversify the racial makeup of schools." This inevitably led to a lot of forced interactions between Blacks and Whites during an extremely turbulent period. You hear about the way things used to be and quickly learn how your life is quite different. Perspective can go a long way.

There were frequent jokes about the way White people acted in school and about how they perceived African Americans. Little tidbits would come up that referenced the inadequate treatment Blacks received in civic life. You also learned that many White people may not be accepting of the modern differences that had transpired in society. It's vital I mention both of my parents were graduates of HBCUs (historically Black colleges and universities), so that may have led to a slightly biased perspective on their part in terms of their overall rhetoric.

By natural means, strong elements of Black culture popped up in our apartment. Because we didn't have access to American television, my uncle would send tapes that included certain shows and movies he knew we'd find appealing. Most notable to me was the film *The Wiz* and episodes of BET's *Video Soul*. For those who may not be familiar, *The Wiz* is a cinematic adaptation of the play by the same name. In a nutshell, it was the Black version of *The Wizard of Oz*. The primary actors in the film were Diana Ross, Michael Jackson, Nipsey Russell, Lena Horne, and Richard Pryor. *Video Soul* was a weekly top twenty-five countdown of the most popular videos in urban music. These were both amazing forms of entertainment to be exposed to, but with respect to the talking points that were floating around, I attempted to look at people at face value, irrespective of race or ethnicity. It was, however, the first time I can recall experiencing a bit of growth through the arts. I'm sure most kids feel that way about their early exposure to creative endeavors, but the more you are exposed to one perspective, the more jaded you can become. It doesn't have to be that way, but that's why I use the word "can." If that's how it occurs, you may have to deconstruct yourself in order to become completely objective.

In a metaphorical sense, it's almost like I was poking the bear within my everyday life just by existing, moving in a way that was contradictory to the norm. Even so, I took it all in without batting an eyelid. I guess I didn't really have much of a choice. Sometimes, life moves so quickly. While so many particulars were being dispersed, one thing that was lacking were stories from the past. Tales that could provide some insight into the lives of my parents prior to them bearing children. Some would come later from my father but not enough to add some real meat in terms of why he had become the man he was. It's possible that parents don't typically provide such information to their kids. Is it conceivable that sharing would have made our dynamic "too personal"? Maybe it's on me for not being more inquisitive, but I always had questions. What was their upbringing like? How did our father propose to our mother? What types of college experiences really helped shape them as adults? Personally, I would have found these stories compelling to hear, but we can never have everything we want.

During our time overseas, I didn't really develop much of a connection with my siblings. I regret not forming a closer bond with them at an early age, but so much of what we experience as children doesn't align with our perspectives as adults. I was mostly confined to my own brain and the events surrounding me. We certainly spent a lot of time together. I guess the art of conversation was lost on us as a five-, four-, and two-year-old. I say that slightly facetiously. It wouldn't be inaccurate to say that I was selfish or at least developing a selfish streak. I undoubtedly had love for them. I mean, most of our major experiences were shared, but our connection wasn't really what one might consider to be emblematic of typical brethren. Whatever they felt meant very little to me during this early period in my life. It hurts me to admit this, but at times, I would even be a bit of a bully to them.

My brother had been held back a year solely because of maturity issues. The fact he attended a German preschool with considerable language barriers had taken a bit of a toll. Whenever things got tense between us, I wouldn't let him hear the end of it. I would poke fun at my sister for a multitude of things, but they were mainly associated with her weight. She wasn't even heavy at all. Even if she had been, it shouldn't have been an excuse for me to use it as a pejorative tactic. I was just acting like an ass. In one instance, my mother left her wallet on top of her car by mistake after leaving our cousin's house and then drove off unknowingly. Inevitably, this caused her to lose the wallet somewhere on the autobahn. I thought the whole thing was hilarious, but to her, it was not, and I undoubtedly mentioned it to her from time to time just to poke fun. I sometimes wonder if I was developing some form of disconnect from general humanity and typical social norms. I'm not sure what that means, but I know what the connotation says to others. It was even around this time that I began to voice the fact I never wanted to have children of my own, which was something that I clearly knew little about other than the fact that the ramifications seemed to be undesirable. I know it's strange to have thought this way as a young child, but I definitely did.

I never took personal jabs at my dad until I was in middle school. Maybe it was because I was a bit intimidated at first, but sometimes when tensions rise, we get a tad more ballsy. As a young kid, most things were fairly copacetic between him and me, so in my mind, it wasn't necessary.

Some toxic traits of mine were absolutely showing. I guess it's possible to chalk it all up to classic sibling behavior, but I definitely went further than I should have. The concept of "kicking a man while he's down" always appealed to me, and I'm not sure why. Maybe this has a lot to do with why I usually found the villains to be more appealing than the heroes. Even now, when it comes to hip hop beef (conflicts) or diss records, I love it when one of the artists goes completely savage on the other. It's a very interesting point of analysis. With my mother being a teacher and my father being in the army, it was as if I was being raised by two heroes, all while possessing an affinity for the dim-witted scoundrel. The ones with darkness associated with their persona. The characters who are unyielding in their efforts to go overboard in order to inflict damage. The Cobra Commanders, Skeletors, and Darth Vaders of the world. I identified with an exotic coolness that I perceived the villains to possess. The darker colors they'd wear were clearly intended to make them seem more devilish, which was cool to me. I'm aware this isn't an uncommon perspective, but like I said, it's interesting to delve into. After all, the villain always has a backstory, and it's never inherently evil. Even as a young child, strident rules never really resonated with me, so I think I was always seeking some type of inner freedom, which usually aligned with the being that was misaligned, even if immoral. Anything to make sense of what I didn't fully identify with. Viewpoints that might put me more at ease and make amends with a world full of subjectiveness. Sometimes our searches are lifelong and go unresolved, but we still must carry on though.

One notable thing I can say about my siblings is that with all we've been through, they are two of the most brilliant humans I've had the pleasure of being around. Although our brains work in different ways, our ability to analyze is uncanny with respect to most others, even if to a fault. These anecdotal pieces are all a part of what birthed me into becoming a bit of a recalcitrant enigma.

4

One of the more seminal moments in my life occurred during the second year of my time living in Europe. I don't quite recall exactly how it all manifested, but somehow, I remember watching part one of the PBS docuseries *Eyes On The Prize*. For those who haven't seen it, the series' premise is to inform the viewer about the early stages of the American civil rights movement, from roughly 1954 to 1965. It was filled with very advanced information, conceptually, for the mind of a five- or six-year-old. But I watched it anyway. I found the subject matter to be fascinating, and that interest of mine remained prevalent throughout the rest of my life.

The Emmett Till segment hit me particularly hard. Its sadism, brutality, and excessive bigotry really resonated in terms of sparking my interest in the Southern African American experience within the US. I watched it alone, with my father occasionally popping in, seemingly unaware of what I was viewing. As a Black child living in Europe, this was my first exposure to the overt racism that had occurred in America. It was also my first major realization of anything being different about myself other than having a different shade of skin. There was a significant cultural divide. The notion of living "across the pond" wasn't as simple as it sounded. The overall experience of being Black would become unique in itself. Obviously, I had heard stories of racism from my parents, but this was the first time I'd been exposed to the type of racism so overt that it included the innocent slaying of a child. It caused me to ask my father if it was better to be White simply because of the immunity the killers experienced after admitting to having committed the crime. I'm sure he was shocked at my inquiry. I was most likely approaching a subject he was not prepared to deal with. He seemed a bit upset I would even broach such a question and quickly replied with, "No . . . and don't you ever ask me that again." So, the issue was dead to me. Being part of such an extreme minority group within a country like Germany would certainly lead to the formation of a slightly off-kilter view of self-identification. It's like you kind of know what's going on, but without knowing much at all. After my father assured me it was certainly NOT better to be White, it really helped with how I looked at myself. And for the time being, it made me feel like I had an ally at home.

In hindsight, it appeared as though his reaction was suppressing something that should have been discussed. But I definitely did not want to talk about such an issue with him, as I knew (even at the age of five or six) that he would be jaded and, therefore, wouldn't present me with an unbiased perspective. It was impartial (or close to it) viewpoints that were going to really aid me in my journey, and I was aware of this from a young age.

5

In Germany, students didn't take the typical "cheese wagon" so commonly associated with the public school transportation system in the United States. We took charter buses. It was nice and relatively comfortable. My earliest memories of riding them involved a young German girl around my age. I don't recall her name, but I definitely remember her being White, blonde, and annoying as hell. The bothersome factor was mainly that she seemed to be obsessed with me because of my Blackness. I don't know this to be factual, but if I got close enough to her, she'd touch my hair and comment on how smooth and pretty my skin was. I've always hated it when people touch my hair without asking; that feeling has never subsided. I guess she could have just been being complimentary, but I sincerely doubt it. On a daily basis, her voice alone would pester me. From the moment I stepped onto the bus, she would call out my name.

"JUSTIN!! JUSTIN!!! COME SIT BY ME IN THE BACK!!" These moments were excruciating. I imagine it was equally grating for the other passengers to have been exposed to. The young lady wasn't remotely subtle, and her actions plagued me (not literally) on the regular. Her bellows echoed throughout the entire bus. I felt I served some sort of "exotic coolness" to her. As if I was a pink poodle. Different enough to be looked at as a pet, yet similar enough to be treated as human, if that makes sense. The nature of the situation was inherently awkward. It was very weird and placed me in an awkward position. My reaction was to blatantly ignore her. The more I turned a blind eye to her affection, the louder she got, which was irritating. But I kind of liked the fact that I was pissing her off. I probably should have just had a chat with her and told her how I felt, but using that type of logic at the age of five isn't common. Internally, I'd smirk at her anger. I found it to be humorous. Maybe it was the villain within?

Now, keep in mind that this is my perspective in hindsight. At the time, it was just plain nauseating. It doesn't take away from the fact that the predicament really screwed with my head. It would have helped if I had been able to have a conversation with my parents about it. I suppose it's possible that I could have, but it didn't feel like it would have been appropriate. Budding developments that are centered around race and human relationships are very important in a young child's life. Being that it was also my first notable interaction with a girl added to its distinctive nature. I would have liked to have discussed it with my mother, even if it was just a surface-level conversation, given that it was a situation dealing with a girl. It's for the exact same reason that I would have wanted to talk about it with my father, in addition to it being a male bonding type of thing. The scenario felt like uncharted territory.

The maternal side of my upbringing was quite different from that of its paternal counterpart, although they did share some similarities. As an educator, much of those early years were based on my mother implementing knowledge. Not so much in terms of "knowledge of self" but just having a grasp on general skills one might expect a first grader to possess. I had no idea having a parent who was supremely invested in their child being able to read well, write with accuracy, and make solid inferences was something that would become a lost art in terms of parenting. But I'm very appreciative of what it sparked within.

Books were always being read to me. This occurred daily. Speak & Spells were in constant use. We reviewed alphabet cards about three times per week. But nothing was being done to ripen my interior well-being, hence the constant independent search for more. I definitely didn't recognize it at the time, but in hindsight, I was always chasing a white rabbit—a fleeting skillset. There weren't any home lessons designed to impact the social/emotional side of development. In hindsight, I've wondered if my mother might have experienced some childhood trauma. If so, that could have led her to act in this manner. Someone can be a great parent and possess a chilling disposition at the same time. It's the understanding of another person's temperament that is key and the one that requires explanations. But outside of my siblings, our family never asked those sorts of questions.

My spirit was numb. I was generally a pretty fun-loving child but finding solace in the misfortune of others was definitely a thing for me. If a student wet their pants or cried, I continued to find those situations to be humorous. My moral perspective didn't have any real direction. Maybe that isn't something parents with young children are tremendously concerned with. Maybe they usually feel like their kids will grow out of it. I wouldn't know at all, as I don't have any kids. But I do feel like discussing morality in detail is a major component when it comes to growing up. It definitely felt like something was missing. Was I actually a mean kid, or was I just a developmental project trying to figure out life?

My mother's academic regiment, in conjunction with her associated expectations, was tight enough to be comparable to my father's rigorous approach. Their primary difference was their demeanor in addressing general conduct. Terry's tactic was to handle with a hands-off attitude. I'd call it casual in nature, but not so much that it seemed like he was completely carefree.

My mother was far more conservative in her methods. In my opinion, everything was "judgy" or a reference to typical ethics (which was oftentimes related to Christianity). It was a very hands-on approach that never addressed the notion of morality being subjective. A major commonality between the two was their reactions being routed by way of a visceral response. Context didn't matter as much as how they felt when facing a given incident. Growing older only made these responses worsen, which caused me to develop a complex that involved conditioning myself to never behave, or respond, as they would. A colder disposition took over for me. Not evil, but maybe more nondescript. Unemotional, not wanting to show much of anything at all. Some would refer to this as suppression, which I can't really argue with at all. It did, however, start to really fit with my developing personality.

Obviously, being a military brat meant bouncing from place to place. Never completely settling anywhere and never getting too attached to any one peer group. Never feeling like you really belonged at a school, on a sports team, or anywhere from a social perspective. On the bright side, you do develop pretty thick skin, and getting too close to situations begins to feel like a taboo reaction. Being an isolationist became appealing, even if it may not have been healthy.

The final memory I have of living in Germany is actually fairly significant, even if it might sound silly to others. Over the course of my time in Europe, I developed a sizable collection of Ninja Turtles action figures. The ones that would be considered classic now, from the cartoon series. I owned all of them! Each Turtle, Master Splinter, The Shredder, April O'Neil, and every one of the side characters. Of course, I took them out of their boxes so they wouldn't have any current value, but to me, those toys served a substantial purpose. I'd play with them on the regular and act like they were fighting one another. Sometimes, I'd even make it seem like they were little football players emulating Joe Montana, Jerry Rice, and many others. I also had a lot of the action figures from the *He-Man* and *ThunderCats* series, but since I owned EVERY one of the Turtles, they meant more to me. I thought they were the coolest fucking toys around, and the fact that each of them had their own facial expression was super unique. I guess you could say I was becoming quite the collector.

We were ready to up and move back to the States. Everything was packed for shipping, and each of us was equipped with whatever we were going to carry onto the plane. We got into the cab that was going to take us right to the airport, and then we'd be on our journey back to the United States. I had my little backpack and my bag full of toys. We exited the cab and made our way into the airport terminal. It was a bittersweet feeling to be leaving such an amazing place, but home is where the heart is. And my home was in the United States. My family had successfully boarded the plane, and we were about to take off. At this point in my life, I had only flown the one time when we made the move to Germany, so this was going to be my second experience flying. Our plane was ready for takeoff, and I recall speaking to my mother. While talking to her, I didn't feel quite right. Something was missing. I turned around and checked to ensure all of my belongings were intact. I looked into my backpack and then went to check for my toys. I rummaged around for a few minutes, but it was clear. The bag was gone. Nowhere to be found. I continued to scurry frantically but to no avail. I had left all of my action figures with the cab driver by mistake, and there was no way to get them back. We couldn't call anyone. There was nobody to reach out to. They were just gone, and I was devastated. I cried for a while, and then the plane took off. At that moment, I was emotionally wounded. I don't recall my mother or father consoling me afterward. They probably had much larger issues to deal with, but part of me felt like my sadness should have resonated with them. Bad things happen, but in the grand scheme of things, this was trivial. It was time to move forward. I had to get over it, and I couldn't be that kid on the plane crying over some little toys. Suck it up and do your best to appear as stoic as possible. Move on to a new plane, no pun intended. Get through it and become better because of it; analysis in hindsight can be beneficial to the soul.

My family left Germany and moved to Fort Leavenworth, Kansas, where we lived for ten months. Kansas was basically a meshed haven of eclectic military families. It wasn't spectacular, nor was it underwhelming. It sat in between, like being in purgatory. It was mostly uneventful, although almost every family on our block had children close to my age. We had a very diverse group of kids consisting of individuals from all over the country. There was always a lot to do because so many playmates were available.

One significant memory I do have of my life in Fort Leavenworth was a foreboding uneasiness was directly related to the possibility of my dad being sent overseas to fight in the Gulf War. Good vs. evil; the United States aiding with allies to combat Saddam Hussein and Iraq. I would readily ask him questions inquiring whether or not he thought he'd be sent into battle, which he would quell on the spot. According to him, since he was technically a student in Kansas, he wasn't really at risk. His words were consoling, especially given the little bit of knowledge I had about deployment and foreign wars as a whole. The real social doozies hadn't hit me yet, but they sure would, and they wouldn't be kind. Living in Kansas was very much a serene prelude to what would ensue.

6

Next destination: DeRidder, Louisiana, where my father would be working at Fort Polk as a lieutenant colonel. DeRidder was a quaint little town. A city in the parish seat of Beauregard Parish, Louisiana. It sits on the west bank of the state, bordering eastern Texas. The parish was named and founded in 1913 after Confederate General P. G. T. Beauregard. Whenever a town, street, school, etc., is named after an individual who fought for the Confederacy, one needs to contemplate the reasons behind the motive. Actually, one should question why any place is named after anyone, but especially if it's someone who fought against the *United* States. I always wondered why my parents didn't brief us kids concerning the differences we would face moving into the Deep South. The cultural shifts were considerable and in need of some coaxing. But there was never any conversation about it. Never any mention of the fact we might have to deal with some real racists, or at least extreme right-wingers with a very racialized agenda.

Our family was certainly going to be exposed to people who had never encountered individuals like us before. Blacks that didn't "stay in their place" or hold a subservient disposition. We moved to a location that had been totally gutted by the civil rights movement, with many of its citizens still seemingly at odds with the 1954 *Brown v. Board of Education* decision. While I had made minor internal progressions, life appeared to be moving backward in time. I heard it all the time in class. Children whispered about their parents' discussions regarding Blacks and Whites going to school together. It was like being Black instantly made you some type of pariah, and if you proved yourself as favorable, then you were just a bit less of a pariah. The strangeness of having to prove oneself solely based on race didn't seem ethical at all. Did the entire state embody a villainous disposition toward people of color? I mean, in the early '90s, Louisiana remained sitting with a polar identity very much in its own space for a litany of reasons. My experiences there still surprise me to this day, but we can't alter the past.

A lot of the street and building names had been aided and carried out by the United Daughters of the Confederacy decades prior, during the early 20th century. These were descendants of Confederate soldiers who sought to immortalize their "heroes" in order for their lost cause to be viewed with nobility. It was common for public property to be named after Confederate veterans or to simply contain the word "Confederate" within their title. You'd also notice the word "dixie" floating around a lot, which doesn't seem so offensive, as it really just references a place, but it still conveys perspectives associated with the old South. I guess the overarching question when it comes to their lost cause becomes, "Noble to whom, and to what cause?" Was their perceived nobility put on a pedestal at the expense of the civil rights of other American citizens? It's just something to think about.

In general, the people of the town embodied what would be considered "Southern hospitality." Just as nice as can be to your face, but there were two sides to the phrase. As a resident, you had to make a decision on which side you identified with. Children were expected to refer to their teachers as either "sir" or "ma'am" (which was quite shocking to me). One of my earliest

Louisiana memories was responding to an adult with, "Yeah." My classmates looked at me like I had dog shit all over my face. The little girl who sat next to me asked why I was being so crass, and I had no idea what she was talking about. It felt like I was living in a new universe. Certain behaviors were considered customary, and an individual's behavior was one of them. But nobody had taught me that behaving differently was key in this new region. Men tipped their hats on the street. Women nodded as they passed. Social dynamics appeared out of whack to me. Everything was confusing.

Optics-wise, DeRidder looked like something out of the old West. I was just waiting on the tumbleweeds to blow past. Even the children held certain state institutions in high regard. One of these was Louisiana State University, or LSU for short. My father used to crack jokes about how it was such a large state school. "They would let anyone and everyone attend, regardless of academic achievement." I casually reiterated this to one of my peers as a joke, and she ran away in tears, telling me how evil I was. I just looked at it as a simple joke. My sense of humor definitely became unique to my demeanor. Even if some others weren't particularly a fan of it, I didn't really care.

There was also an obvious disparity between the Blacks and Whites in the town, or maybe it was more like the haves and the have-nots. The two generally seemed synonymous in terms of them being on opposite ends of everything that encompassed civic life. This was an inequity I had never witnessed before. Most of the Whites who I knew lived in nice-looking one-story homes. They had all of the typical amenities one would expect a house to have: roughly four or five bedrooms, three bathrooms, lots of windows, and a modern-looking kitchen. The neighborhoods felt very safe. This wasn't entirely true, as I grew to know some Whites who were very poor and lived in low-end trailer parks. These were very few and far between, though.

The majority of African Americans I was familiar with lived in houses that likened themselves to an era long forgotten. They looked like shacks resembling pseudo slave quarters. Wooden shanty houses that were set atop cinder blocks. No air conditioning to quell the sweltering Louisiana heat. To me, they looked uninhabitable, but that might just be my arrogance talking. Regardless, it was the socioeconomic division that was glaring.

On my first day of the third grade, my class was required to sit in a semicircle and share our contact information. Standard stuff. Full names, addresses, and phone numbers. During the process, I noticed about half of the class responded with, "We don't have a phone." Most of them looked embarrassed at having to utter such words to a group of about twenty, but I can only imagine how they felt seeing the reactions of the other students, mine included. This moment led me to recognize some of the privileges I had been afforded. It prompted an insecure feeling because I was an outlier in a room of individuals who looked similar to me. I was stunned, mainly because I assumed that everyone had a phone. It was just a typical asset I figured was commonplace. I had no idea it might be considered a luxury for some. So much division. Mostly racial and economic gaps. It was also around this time that I recall my mother telling me that she had a student whose parents told the school's administration they didn't want their son being taught by a Black woman. What a sickening request. Obviously, this sort of request couldn't legitimately be carried out in 1992, but the mere assumption that it was a possibility spoke to the unmitigated gall of certain citizens.

7

The neighborhood my family lived in was called Green Acres. Pretty cheesy, given that there was an early 1970s television series that went by the same name. It was a nice place to raise a family from an outsider's perspective. It gave the appearance of being a gated community without actually being one. The entranceway was slightly regal looking. The homes were nice but typical. Each residence was a one-story unit with a two-car garage. Demographically speaking, it was a mostly White area.

I didn't know everyone the community consisted of, but it was rare to see another brown face, and it was a fairly large neighborhood. The landscape felt like it continued endlessly in all directions. During the day, the warm sun seemed to light up the vicinity in its entirety. I was only aware of one of my African American classmates who lived there, in addition to a childless Black couple my parents were friends with. It was a decent spot, greatly embodying the suburban stereotype. But was it really the "place to be," like the sitcom's theme song stated? Not really. It was more like a southern Levittown. Super "cookie cutter" and assembly line-ish. Similar to how things were in Kansas, but with almost no semblance of diversity. Not remotely conveying the feel of Louisiana I sensed when leaving the wooden gates of Green Acres.

Some of my White friends lived in much larger homes, and I was a tad jealous of their circumstances. This was the first time I had been privy to the way in which more financially fortunate people were living. Military housing in Kansas had been far more uniform, and Green Acres was just sort of blase. I'm not implying I was existing in some form of substandard predicament at all. Not even close to it. But being surrounded by families that owned mini mansions was a unique feeling for me. I didn't love it, nor did I despise it. Mentally, I sat in flux with envy.

The imagery of school infrastructure in DeRidder might have left one in a bit of a conundrum, especially as an outsider. It was like good vs. evil in terms of the manner in which children were able to learn. Some of the facilities seemed completely up to date and adequately serviceable to the general public. However, others appeared to have been less than stellar. Looking as though they might be way behind the times. Antiquated and dilapidated. Possibly constructed quickly and with the intent to be functional on the most basic of levels. I'm not really sure.

The school that I attended upon arrival in the third grade was George Washington Carver Elementary. Named after the brilliant agricultural scientist and inventor who promoted the use of substitutive crops to cotton and procedures to thwart soil depletion. Some people just know him as "The Peanut Guy." I vividly recall some of the adults at the school telling the student body that Carver Elementary had been one of the many "Black schools" constructed during the civil rights movement. Built with the intent to prove the state was making conscious strides to fairly accommodate African Americans in order to deter the push for integrated facilities. I don't fully know if this was accurate, but those were common talking points. Personally, I didn't really care about the reasons behind why it was constructed at that time. I was just trying to exist, and I knew the school was a piece of shit compared to what I had previously experienced. It seemed like the majority of the school building was outdoors and set between massive steel columns. I've heard this type of design is referred to as a "Sunrise School," but it's just something that's been said in passing. We didn't have a typical playground equipped with fun kid stuff but more of a large field to run around in behind the main building. The water fountains and bathrooms were always leaky and contained a toxic scent that seemed septic. The boys' bathroom didn't even have a sufficient number of urinals but did provide us with a massive trough to urinate into. I guess it's pretty funny to think about now, but at the time it seemed completely inappropriate; looking like some sort of relic from *Animal Farm*.

Between ten and fifteen boys would gather around the trough, unzip their pants, and then urinate. Everyone was exposed. Their private parts in full view. It was so fucking strange. Clearly, one can imagine the verbiage that would be floating around during such an instance. General laughter regarding the size and color of the exposed penises was always prevalent. The funniest part was that the boys would often have what we referred to as "piss races." It was a very juvenile practice, to say the least, but two males would stand side by side and then compete to see who could pee the farthest—a completely eye-rolling practice but probably not very surprising given that we were seven and eight. If a student needed to defecate, he certainly shouldn't have expected to have any bathroom doors to aid in privacy. Everything was in plain view—cringeworthy behavior on a daily basis. The conditions forced us to show ourselves in a vulnerable state multiple times per day. I mean, our dicks were out while using the bathroom all of the time. I just dealt with it, as there wasn't really any alternative. I actually ended up getting used to it. For someone like myself, so much of what I was dealing with felt like I had entered into an alternate earthly dimension—a proverbial *Twilight Zone*.

The following year, I attended Pinewood Elementary School.

This is where I recall meeting most of the friends who ended up impacting me in one way or another. According to random elders, Pinewood was one of the old White schools within the district. The facilities were like night and day compared to that of George Washington Carver. Everything was enclosed. The bathrooms and water fountains were decent. No more septic odors or exterior steel railings. Only red brick and sturdy infrastructure. The playground was massive and contained a jungle gym, sandbox, and monkey bars—nothing super memorable, but certainly different from what I had experienced as a third grader. The disparities between the two schools were obvious, but they held a common thread. One was previously considered Black, and the other was considered White. Although both institutions had to educate students of all races, the fact they were still being referred to in an antiquated manner spoke to the general thoughts of the populace. Maybe, given my location, it's not really all that surprising.

8

This was my first and only introduction to the Deep South. It's integral I put the timing of our move into context, as it was roughly one year prior to the gubernatorial run of David Duke. If you're not familiar with Mr. Duke, he's certainly an enigma drenched in right-wing conservatism, racism, veiled bigotry, xenophobia, and tailored suiting. In general, I wouldn't presume politics would enter into the realm of the average third or fourth-grader. But in this case, it permeated our school hallways like a disease. I use the term, "disease," because in this situation, the nature of David Duke's White supremacist message hit at the core of voters. When a hot-button issue affects the voters at their ethical center, the consequences can bleed into the home and then inherently into the minds (and mouths) of children. An environment built on the notion of polar opposites ensued. The concept of good vs. evil was flaring up on a daily basis.

Even as a school-aged child, I observed my fourth-grade peers at Pinewood taking political sides, and I was not an exception. The offspring of the Duke supporters would constantly call the non-Duke supporters "nigger lovers." As one would expect, most of the Black population was anti-Duke. After all, this was a former Ku Klux Klan grand wizard running for the highest political office in the state. One would hope that this would have transitioned into votes, but in the early 1990s, many African Americans living in the south were still reeling from the residual effects of the civil rights movement. Some of my classmates even had relatives that were still working land that was owned by Whites. Regardless of perspective, it wasn't uncommon for voting to be the last thing on the minds of many African Americans. This was built into the culture as a result of generations never being allowed to use their constitutional right. It was sad, to say the least. Nevertheless, this David Duke shit was real. Too real and too divisive.

The lunchroom was a powder keg of explosive rhetoric. Teachers were obviously taking sides as well. Imagine being a Black child and seeing a David Duke sticker on a teacher's vehicle. Obviously, any teacher has the right to support whichever political candidate they choose, but supporting Duke was a bit more telling regarding one's moral compass. I suppose one could claim they were in favor of Duke because of his fiscal agenda or maybe even liking where he stood on an issue like education. But voting for a former Klansman seemed way different. It's not even like he was a "reformed" Klansman or rebuked his former organization. This man was a full-fledged White supremacist who was running for governor of Louisiana. I wondered if there was any middle ground for someone like Duke from a moral perspective. Was it possible for someone to support the ideals of the KKK and be a good person on the inside? A man from the most non-marginalized, dominant group in America was readily arguing for the sake of White pride. It just didn't seem okay to me. Everything was wacky.

At one point during the election, my father and I took a mini vacation across the state to New Orleans. If I remember correctly, it was for a Taekwondo tournament in which I was competing. The event was underwhelming, as I recall, but one of the standout aspects of the trip was there being David Duke banners placed across the city in predominantly African American areas. Even as a kid, l was shocked and disgusted with this. I couldn't figure out why Duke's political banners had been hung in these locations. Something about it seemed corrupt. Had members of Duke's street team put them in Black neighborhoods as an attempt to be insulting? Was it all just a joke? Were African Americans actually supporting an extreme right-wing candidate who had previously been a grand wizard in the KKK? My guess would be no.

Nevertheless, the question ran through my head. Scary hours were upon us. Hell, I guess this would have been true regardless of the era within American history. Couldn't someone from the federal government step in and prevent such a person from running for office? Clearly, I didn't understand how the government worked. Even though these issues appeared to be relegated to the South, weren't we supposed to be a united country? This was never really the case. I know it's a lofty goal, but having the former head of a domestic terrorist organization taken seriously didn't seem like something that should have been able to occur during the late 20th century, at least not in the United States of America. Obviously I was confused about a lot, but maybe I was the crazy one. Nothing really seemed certain. From a moral perspective, has the nation been lost throughout its entire existence?

When I returned home from New Orleans, I noticed things changing amongst the students on the playground. If there was ever a conflict between kids of "opposite" races, the song, "Fight, Fight, Black versus White! If White don't win, we all jump in!" would arise. This was a weekly thing. Maybe even more often. I'd probably ballpark it as occurring about twice a week. And for a child like myself, I was always caught in the middle. The social dynamics were so polar. I was clearly Black and proud of it. However, I was from a middle-class family that was "supposed" to be poor. Not poor because of situational factors but poor because we were Black. Being poor and Black was the status quo in that region. It was expected of us to speak with poor grammar, watch television shows with a mostly Black cast, listen exclusively to hip-hop and R&B music, and be preoccupied with sports like football and basketball. All typical Black stereotypes. Very ignorant points of view. In reality, this wasn't remotely true, but the perceptions from others were real. No ethnic group acts and moves as a monolith. The thoughts from so many assumed people would stick to "their own" and never venture outside of their little bubble.

So much of who I was becoming placed me between both groups. It was a case of "not-so-spoken" identity. In past generations, the races were expected to act according to their stereotypical role. This assumption would clearly place an individual of mixed or biracial identity at a crossroads. I wasn't biracial, but I was beginning to feel a bit "bicultural," if that makes any sense. Someone who was mixed would have been expected to choose between one or the other. This didn't have to be the case when I was growing up, but the overall theory behind it was still prevalent. As a Black child who didn't fit into any preconceived molds, I was still placed in an awkward position derived from conventional perspectives. Personally, I didn't feel as though these labels were warranted at all. They didn't allow the individual to grow or even prove themself within a merit-based context. It was all about projecting based on what one had previously been exposed to, even if only through the lens of the media. People were being judged without any accurate pretense. As someone subjected to this judgment, it was particularly off-putting. The struggle to get through it wouldn't be easy, but it would be necessary.

9

I guess one could say my palate was pretty eclectic. This was antithetical to what the average person would expect from someone like me, especially during the early '90s. I was into sports and just beginning to become ingratiated in the world of hip-hop. My parents consistently shared urban music with us by the likes of Michael Jackson, Prince, Anita Baker, Chuck Brown, and Luther Vandross. I'm using the term "urban" to differentiate between artists who have a mostly Black following versus those who have a mainly White following. It isn't an accurate term, as one could be Black and create blatant pop music while still being lumped in with urban artists. It's a sad and unfortunate reality that is rooted in keeping individuals placed in a box.

In addition to those acts, in my own time, I listened to the likes of Def Leppard, Madonna, Phil Collins, George Michael, Garth Brooks, and Taylor Dane. I watched *The Fresh Prince of Bel-Air*, *Martin*, and *Family Matters*. I was also very into *90210*, *Roseanne*, *Home Improvement*, and *Cheers*. My television bible was "*Saved by the Bell*. Films like *Rocky V* and *Mannequin* were staples in my home. But then again, so were, *Boyz n the Hood* and *Malcolm X*. I played tennis and got straight A's. Both of my parents were gainfully employed. My family wasn't well off, but we lived pretty decently. These contradicting elements in regard to perceived norms went against the typical social order, and my teachers were not shy about letting me know this. They would often overhear my conversations and raise their eyebrows at my remarks. It was woven into their social thread to be anxious or at least startled by this type of fabric.

Once again, these were the simplest prognostications. They weren't based on reality. The assumptions relied on using a formula to judge people in terms of what they should or shouldn't become aligned with. I didn't adhere to most of these notions, but I still had to be aware they existed. Not buying into them, yet knowing that others felt as though they were gospel, became a significant battle.

10

My fourth-grade class took field trips to local plantations. I don't recall any specific names. Only general experiences. The educators, as well as the tour guides, were not shy about using the term "glory" when referencing the nature and history of the plantations. Never any mention of the literal horrors that occurred on the property. Never anything referencing the misogyny that kept the women in their place, irrespective of race. Just "glory" used over and over again. The facade seemed to be based in willful ignorance and certainly a bit of intentional White supremacy. The way they pushed their narrative left me harboring a bit of vitriol for that perspective. The intentions seemed rooted in evil but almost like they didn't know any other way to express what they saw as being historically accurate. Their schools and social systems had clearly failed them.

The tour guide paraded our class around the plantation grounds. There were grandiose explanations of the design schemes. Very explicit portrayals of the landscaping. Meticulous depictions of cannons that had been constructed as defense mechanisms during the Civil War. We toured the "big house" (the palatial property on the land) at a snail's pace. Scouring each and every room in order to digest all positive aspects imaginable.

While in the kitchen, our guide removed much of the silverware to showcase the craftsmanship and attention to detail that went into their formation.

The level of optimism behind the entire process was incongruous with reality. I'm not saying these types of colossal plantations aren't gorgeous in nature. They are striking in so many ways. The amount of wealth they produced was exuberant, without a doubt. There was just so much that was being eliminated from the overall testimony. Despite the fact that we were no older than nine or ten, we had the right to know what had occurred on these grounds. I'm by no means suggesting that kids our age should have been briefed with EVERY single horror that could have been prevalent on such a plantation. But if one paints a picture rampant with half-truths or even untruths, then the knowledge base of the children is heavily skewed in one direction. We had the right to know how such affluence was accumulated. Shouldn't we have at least been able to tour the slave quarters? Or had they been torn down in order to erase any semblance of guilt? I can't answer that question accurately, as it's not something our class was exposed to. All I know is that the portrait that was produced in our presence was providing us with fake news. Fifty percent of the story. Maybe even less than that. After all, these homes and their respective lands are works of art.

Plantations are, without a doubt, grandiose architectural constructions. But why not share with us the fact that these grounds were cash-crop factories? Assembly lines for human concubines that were rooted in America's original sin. Kids are capable of comprehending so much more than adults give them credit for. From a purely historical standpoint, after the abolishment of the international slave trade in 1808, these Deep Southern facilities were even greater contributors to the practice of human trafficking than they had been prior to the eradication of the worldwide involvement in this devilish scheme. No longer would slave ships be docking at ports on the east coast or in the Gulf. The buying and selling of human beings within the southern region experienced a massive boom, which altered the overall experiences with respect to plantation life. The common trope of the era was that it was far worse to be held in bondage in the Deep South, as opposed to being a slave in a state like Maryland or Virginia (which isn't to remotely imply that any type of slave living was "decent").

So, here we were, touring a Louisiana plantation, where life would have been excruciating for its slaves. "Excruciating" may be an understatement. Maybe "hellish" is a more appropriate phrase. Either way, the truth was eluding us as children.

Of course, we have to view the inner workings of a 19th-century plantation through a lens that reflects the time period. But that would imply there wasn't an active movement in place to abolish the practice of slavery. So, we received a portion of the truth. Would any of us benefit from experiencing half of an artistic piece, or should we be able to interpret them as a whole? If Leonardo da Vinci had stopped midway through the process of painting the *Mona Lisa*, would it mean as much to society? Would the ceiling of the Sistine Chapel appear as immaculate if Michelangelo hadn't completed it? Shouldn't we all be allowed to interpret notable entities without a skewed perspective? If one gets to pick and choose what parts of history are exemplified, then they have a better chance at controlling a narrative. So many students grow up only being exposed to whatever their state's education system deems appropriate. Such subjectivity when dealing with young minds doesn't always do them justice, and then they can end up struggling with the truth.

On another occasion, my class took a different type of field trip to a local swamp. This was intended to help us become "one with nature" and to learn the practical skill of fishing. Nothing historically based at all. Mildly educational, to say the least. Nobody seemed to care that the swamp was on someone's property. While our class was fishing, some of the children who lived there came down to greet us. More specifically, they came to greet the Black kids "on their property." They specifically told the African American children, "if the niggers didn't leave right away, they would be shot with their father's double barrel." None of my classmates seemed to give much credence to the threat, but I recall being slightly terrified. I don't have any idea how the swamp kids managed to circumvent our teacher. Maybe it was just a regular harmless occurrence to her? All I know is that if the education system places racist code into its actions, it becomes difficult to get rid of. It permeates people's minds and convinces them that whatever is being projected is the norm.

This was the early 1990s, but the depths of the Lost Cause narrative were cutting deep into southern society. Many genuinely felt as though the ways of the old south were being lost within modern civilization. Some thought the racial hierarchy of the past wasn't actually racist but a gentile system ordained by God. It was all peculiar to me. This was also the first time I'd seen individuals brazenly flying the Confederate flag. There appeared to be a clear correlation between the symbolic nature of the flag and desire to preserve antiquated ways. It wasn't like it was just one or two people either. It was rampant within the town of DeRidder. Driving through the streets just to fulfill typical duties would lead one to see this flag in front of homes and on vehicles maybe five or six times per day. The attempt to preserve systems and ideals of the past seemed to be intrinsic to much of the population. And it was often at the expense of others. Keep in mind, I was coming off the heels of living in Germany and then in Kansas. Both were far more progressive environments than what I was dealing with at the moment.

11

At the time, I had a crush on a brunette who sat across from me in class. Her name was Erin. I guess you could say we had a typical friendship. All of our interactions were fairly normal for a couple of fourth graders. We'd flirt back and forth, sometimes exchanging jokes. I would let her cheat off me during our weekly multiplication exams. She had flushed cheeks, a huge smile, and very catlike eyes. Her most distinctive feature was her exceptionally long ponytail. It extended from the back of her head down beneath her waist, and it was always tied so tightly. There was no way that thing was coming undone. She'd keep about four or five rubber bands in it and usually a barrette. When we'd be in line for the water fountain, I would lightly tug on it for fun. Erin found it comical, so it was clearly a consensual joke. If I was ever in front of her, she would occasionally run her fingers through the back of my hair. I really didn't mind at all. Maybe it was because my hair wasn't particularly long at the time. If someone did that to me now, I'd be fuming.

One day, she hit me with some rhetoric that would resonate with me forever. We were goofing off during some down time and she said, "Ya know, I really like you, and I would love to jump right over this desk right now and give you a kiss, *if* you were White." My head jerked back in shock. I had to do a mental double take. In hindsight, it's kind of funny. But at the time, it was a real "what the fuck?" type of moment. Or "did I really hear that shit?" The real kicker was that she was okay uttering it out loud in front of our classmates. I would have thought it would be something to keep to oneself, if that's how she really felt. In that moment, social and racial perceptions took precedence over visceral ones. Nurture had far surpassed nature, at the age of nine.

I'm not sure if it would come as a surprise to most or not, but those types of racial talking points were common once kids started to express interest in one another. Or at least they were common where I was living. Erin's words clearly stuck with me, but in the moment they were brushed aside and disregarded as commonplace. I wasn't even particularly infuriated by the blatant racism that had just been projected toward me. Surprised, yes, but not incensed. It was like I was becoming numb all over again. Obviously no kid wants to completely act out because someone says something to them they don't like. It's important to embody a level of restraint with respect to the words of others. But the fact what Erin said wasn't jaw dropping to the other students was quite telling. Nobody was surprised. Some even giggled a bit. She and I actually continued to be friends, although I didn't look at her the same afterward. My flirtations definitely ceased. At some point, you just kind of learn to let some shit fall by the wayside, even when you shouldn't.

Other than having a low-key fondness for Erin, I had a similar affinity for another girl who was in the same class. Her name was Ashley. I'm not trying to present myself as some sort of pre-pubescent Don Juan, but I'm just explaining pertinent aspects to the social dynamic I experienced. My relationship with Ashley was quite similar to what I had with Erin, with the only glaring difference being that Ashley was Black. Although very young, she embodied similar aesthetic qualities to that of Tatyana Ali, who played Ashley Banks on *The Fresh Prince of Bel-*

Air. Light hazel-colored skin like an autumn leaf. Long legs, shoulder-length hair, and mahogany brown eyes. She had an electrifying smile and teeth that were as white as freshly cleaned piano keys. Ashley was tall for her age. Definitely taller than most of us and seemed almost Amazonian at the time. I've never been one to pay close attention to a person's fingernails, but even at the age of nine, hers stood out to me. They always appeared to be movie-star ready, with a pinkish tone that resembled flower petals.

We played around with one another a lot during class and at recess, especially when I wasn't too engaged with the other boys playing football or talking sports. One notable difference between my relationships with Ashley in comparison to Erin was that Ashley would invite me over to play after school. Our play dates mostly consisted of the two of us playing Nintendo for an hour or so. Usually it was *Super Contra*, *Super Mario Bros. 3*, or *Tetris*. Her parents were cordial toward me and never asked any questions. My parents didn't inquire about our relationship either. I always wondered why they didn't. It seems like such a common inquiry to ask your kid something like, "So what's going on with you and 'whoever'?" But it never came up. Not then or in the future with other girls. Furthermore, our classmates didn't make any inquiries, which was the complete opposite of how they treated my friendship with Erin. Maybe the whole race thing was at the highest end of polar discussion points to my peer group.

Another individual I established a close connection with while living in Louisiana was a boy named Clark. He and I (as well as Ashley and Erin) had become friends as a part of the same group that toured those "splendid" plantations. Clark was chill and had a great sense of humor. He was a White kid I perceived as acting a tad on the feminine side compared to other boys. I don't mean that to be derogatory but just how I viewed him. It didn't really matter to me anyway. I never confirmed this, but he seemed like the kind of kid who had lived in DeRidder for a while. Longer than me at least. I'm really only attributing this to his thick Southern accent and the fact most of the town's residents were mainstays in the area. His family lived about 15 minutes from us, so it wasn't like we had the regular opportunity to play together after school or anything. One day, he asked if I'd be interested in coming over to his place for a sleepover. As a ten-year-old, sleepovers were always enjoyable gatherings. Any chance to get away from your own house was appealing. Typically, the other kids' parents were overly accommodating as well, so it was really a win for all parties involved. I was thrilled by the invite and agreed. Our parents eventually exchanged contact information, and the wheels were in motion.

Once the night arrived, it was a great time. We horsed around outside for a while and then ordered dinner from Pizza Hut. Although Pizza Hut isn't exactly a delicacy, it certainly seems like it is when you're young. After eating, his family and I made our way to the local Blockbuster to rent a movie. For those who aren't aware, Blockbuster was one of the classic video rental stores during the '80s and '90s. Our movie pick was *Ladybugs* starring Rodney Dangerfield and Jackée Harry. A cute comedy about a coach of a struggling girls' soccer team who convinces his future son in law to dress as a girl and take the team out of the gutter to become champions. In one particular scene, Rodney and Jackee's characters are arguing about who's the best player on the team. Rodney thinks that it's a White girl, while Jackée favors a Black kid. In one of her lines, she says, "You know that Black people are the best at sports. We're the fastest runners, the best at track, the best at boxing, the best at basketball, the best at football, you name it . . ." It's a funny quote, for sure. After the scene, Clark's mother looked over at me and said, "Did ya hear that, Justin?" It was humorous, but I wasn't really sure if I should be laughing. Ultimately, I chalked it up to just being a frivolous reference to a playful moment in a lighthearted comedy. Sometimes jokes are just jokes, and other times they carry some weight.

The following day, Clark and I woke up, ate breakfast, and then went out to play on his trampoline. His mother's comment from the night before was still sitting with me, but more so because it was funny. In no way did I think she had malicious intent. Nor did I think she harbored any racist feelings. It was, however, an uncomfortable moment. Maybe because I was the lone Black child as a guest in a White household. I could have easily been getting irritated with hearing race being mentioned when it seemed like it shouldn't be. Humor was one thing, but real feelings were another. Separating racist jokes from racist intent isn't always the most straightforward process. Anyhow, Clark and I continued to jump around and chat. We discussed the latest schoolyard bullshit, which was always entertaining, even though we would probably sound like idiotic drama kings to others. Clark brought up how he had heard I had a crush on both Erin and Ashley. I was a tad embarrassed. Not because of anything regarding them but just because people knew I had a little thing for a few girls. I was honest and admitted I liked them and he followed up with, "Well, you know it isn't right for Black boys to like White girls. And I heard that Erin likes you too, and you know that's also wrong." I didn't even acknowledge his comment. I just kept jumping. His sole focus was on Erin, and it was because she was White. These micro-aggressions were draining. His comment didn't alter our friendship at all, and in recent years, he and I have talked about the issue. He was just reiterating the same points he had heard from our peers. It's all understandable now, but at the time it contributed to some proliferating confusion.

As my memory serves me, there was one other notable student that I remember from my time in Louisiana. I use the term "notable" as it pertains to fairly acute memories on race relations. She wasn't part of my class, but I think she was a member of the class a few rooms down the hallway. This is a bit hazy, so the accuracy could be questionable. But the primary factors within my memory bank are ironclad. The young lady's name was Tracy. She was Asian, and more specifically, she was of Chinese descent. This was rare for the DeRidder, Louisiana, landscape from an ethnic perspective in 1993. I only saw her from afar, but even with that being the case, I remember thinking she embodied an aesthetic quality that I wasn't used to. She was beautiful but different. In the mind of a nine-year-old me, a girl simply appearing different was sometimes enough to incite minor feelings of affection. As I reminisce, I recall mentioning to one of my friends that I thought she was attractive, and his visceral response was unforgettable, to say the least. He explicitly said to me, "DUDE, YOU CANNOT TALK TO HER! HER DAD HATES BLACK BOYS! HE USES THE 'N' WORD ALL OF THE TIME!" Honestly, I couldn't believe what I was hearing. Although I had already been exposed to such rhetoric, it never ceased to shock me. And this time it was stemming from someone who was Asian. The consistent judgments based exclusively on color constantly appeared to demean humanity as a whole. It was like nobody was ever able to just be who they were because their race was the catalyst for any ensuing judgments. I never spoke to Tracy, possibly out of fear. Maybe it was because we were in different classes, and I didn't want to make that type of social leap. I know that I didn't want to make a fool out of myself. Maybe I was actually worried her dad would go off the rails and attempt to cause harm. Nevertheless, the toxic association my friend had attached to Tracy's father left a bad taste in my mouth. I was beginning to learn that general prejudiced attitudes might have been less of the exception and more of the rule.

I wouldn't have been surprised if some of my White classmates had parents who were members of the Council of Conservative Citizens. To give some context, the organization is a modern offshoot of the White Citizens' Council that did so much to hinder the integration movement during the 1960s. Maybe some would have been sympathetic to feelings that were harbored in Judge Thomas Brady's 1954 piece, "Black Monday" (referencing the "Dixiecratic" point of view on the Monday following the Supreme Court's *Brown v. Board of Education* decision). I only make this slight suggestion because the sentiment was prevalent in the atmosphere like a light mist. It was impossible to get rid of. Students, even at ages nine or ten, knew it was social suicide for a White girl to openly express any non-platonic feelings for a Black boy. The same was true if an African American male felt any type of way about a White girl. You'd be called out instantly. Laughed at. Gawked at. The rumor mill would spread throughout the school before the end of the day. And this was all based on color and the perception of differentiated cultures. Micro and macro aggressions galore. Coincidentally, you never heard anything about White boys having crushes on Black girls or the reverse. I'm sure it occurred, but it seemed like an even more uncomfortable reality to talk about openly. It was almost like this nonsense was an extreme derivative of postbellum racial stereotypes. And the only way these predisposed feelings would manifest themselves in children would be if they came straight from the parents. This naturally implies that prejudiced rhetoric was cyclical. It was a tragic reality, but there was little time to dwell on it at the moment. I had to just keep progressing.

12

On the reverse side of engagements, where race became a factor, was the fact that my family had developed a close relationship with another family, the Harringtons. I don't quite remember how we were connected, but I think it's because my sister was friends with their youngest child, Nicole. Actually, it's possible that my mom was one of Nicole's teachers and developed a bond with her mother. Regardless, a relationship ensued. Shayna and Nicole were about the same age, but their other two children, whose names I don't recall, were teenage boys. They were a White family who lived in a neighborhood that seemed more affluent than ours. This caused more envy within myself but nothing major. The ties between us stood out to me because they seemed so genuine. With so much centering around racial dynamics down there, being at the Harringtons' was completely reassuring. Humanity actually had a chance. Everything was rooted in good fun, solid morality, and familial connections.

They had an in-ground pool, which was a first for me in terms of my exposure to that type of amenity. When we moved to Louisiana, I didn't know how to swim and was actually pretty scared of water. One day, one of the older brothers pushed me in unassumingly when I was standing by the edge. I was livid, but it helped me overcome my fear of water. Kudos to him.

There was one night that I remember my dad coming over to join everyone and suggesting we all watch the super low-key martial arts classic *Best of the Best*. The Harringtons obliged. I had never seen this movie before, but Terry was completely engaged and pretty excited. His enthusiasm rubbed off on everyone else in the room, especially myself. It was such a fun time, and the first time I recall my family hanging out with a group of Whites. The vibes in the room were so easygoing and nonchalant. In turn, *Best of the Best* ended up becoming one of my all-time favorite movies. I love almost everything about it, but maybe part of my affinity is due to the initial feeling I received from the moment at hand. Unfortunately, this little beacon of hope wasn't indicative of the way most relationships would be reflected in my world.

13

Living in Louisiana really helped provide context to people's outlooks on interracial bonds, even within platonic friendships and/or civic life. At its most basic level, it delivered a framework into the views held by lots of southerners. The thing about said relationships is that they often seem more complex than they really are. They *can* run deep in terms of the ethnic dynamics at play, or they can entirely lack racial complexity and be solely based on having like-minded qualities. From a historically sociological perspective, some White women fetishized Black men. During the antebellum period, slave narratives and accounts that focused on this dynamic would have challenged the dominant perspectives of White womanhood, and therefore would have been subdued. Some Black men fetishized White women. On occasion, Black women would do it to White men and vice versa. There are obviously levels to all of this, but people can, and will, fetishize any and everything. The reasons behind it all are what make it so noteworthy.

For the duration of the antebellum period in the South, White women and Black men were generally kept away from one another by the powers in place. White women were put on a pedestal and looked at as pillars of virtue, while Black men who worked as laborers were viewed as childlike and brutish. White men were commonly seen as "masters of the universe" (even if they didn't possess any substantial wealth, they still benefited from being White and male). Female slaves were considered pieces of property to be used at the White man's disposal. Men and women who worked in the "big house" were also property to be exploited for their domestic skills.

Throughout the postbellum era, some perspectives (especially from political and social standpoints) were intentionally altered to paint the Black man as a menace to society who needed to be controlled, while White women were stereotyped as pristine beings who could never be approached, other than by a White man. In many areas of the American South, if a Black male made advances toward her, he was instantly vilified, murdered, or viciously maimed. At the very least his motives would be the subject of interrogation. He was portrayed as lusting after something he was not supposed to have. What do you think the song "Strange Fruit" is about? "Black bodies swinging in the summer breeze . . ." It's important to note during the late 19th and early 20th centuries, the United States was the only first-world nation where human beings were literally burned at the stake for such societal misgivings. Not for committing a felony or a misdemeanor. But something that merely went against the typical social order of the area. This could occur regardless of whether or not the advances were consensual. One could even fast-forward to 2015, when a White supremacist gunman decimated nine Black churchgoers in Charleston, South Carolina. While committing this disgraceful act, he said, "You rape our women and you are taking over our country."

Venomous viewpoints often linger. If a White woman made a play at a Black man, she was portrayed as a tainted tramp who was also embracing the forbidden fruit narrative (or the scenario was kept as clandestine as possible). If an African American woman wanted to be with a White man, certain segments of society would refer to her as a power-hungry jezebel. And if the reverse scenario occurred, he was construed as just wanting to use her for her body, as if she was a possession. These projections stick to the ribs of society. Sometimes they are true. Obviously not 100 percent of the time. They would most likely be super rare, but these purposeful falsehoods rest in the underbelly of our culture. Many individuals love to believe whatever is most convenient to push their most comfortable narrative.

One could simply look at how the adult film industry plays on all of this while raking in billions of dollars in revenue. Conversely, the fetish element, with respect to races of people, can be very much nonexistent. Personal preferences can be prevalent just as easily as they can be absent. In terms of relationships, I never understood why modernized people put so much effort into caring about the choices, and lives, of others. Maybe that's just part of the human condition. And when it comes to race (specifically between Blacks and Whites), so much of said condition is based on interactions from the past this nation has done an extremely shitty job reconciling. I'm obviously aware that America consists of a multitude of ethnicities, but I'm simplifying the observation to make an acute point of analysis. Much of this happened over 140 years ago, but the more you learn the more you realize that a lot of people's thoughts and actions haven't progressed much. The trickle-down effect from the past is real, and hence the obvious truth behind the concept of systemic racism. When you begin to notice heinous and oppressive viewpoints bleeding into the interaction of the youth, it becomes eye opening. Those who are trying to grow as "little humans" become affected by a cancerous ideology that has been bestowed upon them. Sometimes intentionally and sometimes as a byproduct of culture. Either way, it can stifle young minds. These are talking points that large segments of America would prefer not be thought about, scrutinized, or discussed. The legendary Tupac Shakur once profoundly said, "America eats its babies."

14

It's not like things were *all* bad down there. Racism was a cultural mainstay, but this period really helped me develop internally in some ways. I was garnering a hefty interest in athletics, which led to a disproportionate relationship with my father, as he was an avid sports fan. Every day I'd come home from school and work on my homework while watching classic football games on ESPN's *NFL Films Presents*. He and I would discuss some of the iconic players involved. It gave him a chance to harken back to his past as a football fan from the '70s and '80s, and conversely it gave me a chance to bond with him regarding a fresh interest of mine.

Terry would let me join him at the local gym a few days a week, which was actually a bit risky. The policy was that no one under the age of 16 was allowed, but I was granted permission to go on the condition I didn't use any of the weights. The owner wasn't super happy about it, but he let it slide nonetheless. I was only allowed to do light running, pushups, pullups, and dips. Body weight type stuff. This developed an attention to fitness and aesthetics that would become a staple within myself. I've always been a bit undersized. Short, but with the ability to hold on to solid lean muscle. I've never been particularly insecure about my height. But maybe that's because I've convinced myself it wasn't a big deal, I wasn't THAT short. There were always others who were smaller, but exercising regularly gave me an opportunity to exude some form of athletic prowess, even if the benefits were predominantly personal. It had its drawbacks, as I would sometimes be overly concerned with appearances and come off as shallow or pretentious. In my head, it was better to be too concerned with all of that than not concerned enough. My dad once said something that would stick with me forever. He told me, "It's best to never stop training; always make your most concentrated effort to do so on the days that you most want to avoid it." Powerful words in my opinion.

Eventually, the owner of the gym became even more okay with me working out from time to time. He was always reluctant, but since he was a friend of my dad's he was more chill than he probably would have otherwise been. Their biggest concern was that having a child exercising at a reputable fitness establishment could lead to some sort of situation where they were liable. I can't blame them for that at all, but maybe I'm using the term "reputable" too loosely? I mean, it was a little gym in the backwoods behind a trailer park. Probably off of the grid for most people. Someone probably could have died in that gym and the authorities wouldn't be notified for over a week. I say that in complete jest. It might sound a bit judgy, but that's how I viewed it at the time.

One evening, my father and I showed up for a quick workout. Right during prime time for the television networks. I hit the treadmill and he went straight for the weight sets. There was a group of TVs above each of the treadmills so the runners could pass the time with some entertainment, especially if they hadn't brought a Walkman with them. I flipped through the channels until I landed on Fox, and just as luck would have it, *90210* was on. Perfect! This just happened to be the episode where Dylan McKay's father gets murdered. I was maybe five minutes into my jog when all of a sudden, BOOOOOM! Dylan's dad's car blew up in surprising fashion. I was so shocked by what happened, I stutter-stepped on the treadmill and then proceeded to fall forward. My head abrasively landed against the fast revolving conveyor, which then threw me backwards into a sturdy partition. Another boom ensued, but it was caused by *my* body. I was hurt, but not badly. My adrenaline prompted me to get up and act like nothing had happened, but everyone made their way back to the treadmill area to inquire. I was embarrassed, but also thought it was kind of funny at the same time. I got up scratching my head and holding my back. My dad came to check on me, and once it was clear that I was okay, we both went back to working out. The gym owner never even made an issue out of it, and I have no idea why he didn't. Oh well. No harm, no foul, I guess?

Outside of the interpersonal bullshit that was going on, and the bits of release therapy that I got from spending time with my father, school recess was quite the safe space for me. All of that "Black vs. White" fuckery went out the window because the boys settled things on the football field. I suppose that's when I noticed things becoming more merit based on some level. If you showed out, then you got respect, at least in the short term. One of the best things about outdoor recreational life in Louisiana was that the temperature in the afternoon was typically ideal. In addition to developing my athletic side, it also helped drive my artistic sensibilities. Sometimes personal growth can occur where you least expect it.

On certain days, when I didn't feel like engaging with sports, I'd confine myself to the outside margins of the playground. Just walking around with my tape player, typically listening to Michael Jackson records. Mainly the albums *Bad* and *Dangerous*. I'd dissect the fuck out of them too. The intense blending of pop and urban sonics. Heavy basslines, guitar solos, and wild vocals. Wild, but with the most control I'd ever heard. It was almost like the mixture of styles Michael possessed became the soundtrack to my life, as my life was a merger of so many things in itself.

One thing I noticed was intrinsically missing was a connection to an urban lifestyle. And my African American peers were not shy about making this known. After all, I was the only Black kid in my class that was not from an economically disenfranchised neighborhood. Although my parents (my father specifically) had exposed me to urban and hip-hop culture, it was kind of like the watered down version. At this point, the most hip hop I'd really listened to was the Salt-N-Pepa album *A Salt with A Deadly Pepa*. But something new was brewing. . . .

15

A new rap album was completely re-shaping the sound of hip hop. It was Dr. Dre's *The Chronic*. A collaborative piece with a vastly altered approach to sampling, production, mixing, and lyrical delivery. A sonic vessel into the world of inner-city Los Angeles following the incendiary Watts riots. The project wasn't remotely on my radar when it dropped, as we weren't exposed to gangsta rap in my home, but that would all quickly change.

On one occasion during class, most of the Black kids took their turns clowning me because I didn't know the lyrics to "Nuthin' but a 'G' Thang" word for word. Hell, I hadn't even heard of the song at that point. It was also becoming increasingly popular for the students to quote lines from the song "Deeez Nuuuts." I was essentially bullied into finding a way to purchase the cassette tape. I'm using the term "bullied" in a slightly sarcastic manner, as none of the treatment I received was malicious but more like kids having lighthearted fun at the expense of someone else. This form of pseudo mal-intent ended up having a positive effect on my musical palate. Once I was able to get my hands on the album, I was intoxicated by the vibes. One of my friends made me a bootlegged copy titled "R&B Radio Jamz" (just to keep my parents at bay). The feeling I got when listening to that record was similar to the way I was moved by Michael, but in an opposing manner. The unapologetic references to drugs, booze, and women were the furthest thing from anything I had been exposed to up until that point. My father's side of the family was from Prince George's County, Maryland, so it wasn't like I was completely aloof from inner-city staples. The music became another realm of escapism for me. But once the school bell rang, it was back to reality. Slowly, I was beginning to recognize that having outlets to turn to would help me deal with any real-life turmoil.

Another thought-provoking caveat associated with this newfound exposure to gangsta rap was that it was the first time that I had heard the word "nigga" used regularly. I was well aware of the vitriol that came with Whites using "nigger" when referencing African Americans, but this new type of slang threw me for a bit of a loop. The members of my father's side of our family didn't even use this term. Not around the kids anyway. I was confused, but not enough to hinder any enjoyment in the art form. Individuals from different demographics use all sorts of vernacular others aren't used to, so I kind of chalked it up to people just being from different areas, and therefore speaking in a colloquial sense that reflected their culture. I wasn't bothered at all by its use, but I did often wonder what White kids would think when they heard it.

Even though the word was merely a derivative of "nigger," and therefore not the same, it was close enough for me to assume that people would naturally conflate the two. It wasn't until I was much older and had studied some sociology that I began to understand where its marginalized usage came from.

Between the 17th and late 19th centuries in the United States, the word "nigger" was commonly spoken to reference anyone who was African American. It was so pervasive within the English language in the States that it wasn't even solely used as an insult. A lot of the time it was intended to be a synonym for calling someone "Black," "colored," or a "negro." But because an explicitly punitive tinge was associated with the word, it still manifested a feeling of being proverbially thrashed every time it was uttered. If a White man was attempting to get the attention of a Black person who had congregated within a group, he might say, "Hey, nigger!" It wouldn't be uncommon for the entire group to turn around, assuming one of them was being addressed. That's how prevalent this deeply detestable word was being spoken. At one point, it had even evolved into being used as "niggra" or even "niggress" (in reference to an African American woman). It isn't pretty, or enjoyable to discuss, but it was a reality, especially within the South. The word was so ubiquitous that Blacks began to use the term to refer to one another, which is understandable given its relentless usage from Whites. One wouldn't have even had to be racist to assume the slur wasn't intentionally punitive.

Once slavery was abolished, and the ensuing demise of Reconstruction had occurred, African Americans began to slowly migrate north in search of better and more equitably fair opportunities. During this arduous process of relocation, language was never left behind. This was The Great Migration.

After Blacks had grown accustomed to using "nigger" to refer to each other while having previously existed in a system based on chattel slavery (as it had been cyclically used by Whites for centuries as a pejorative term) it became a phrase that was recurrently tossed around within African American groups in urban centers. This is where the slang element came into play. Over time, gone was the "er" replaced with an "a." That minor alteration completely deviated the context in terms of its offensive nature. With that being said, the newly evolved expression was not customarily used in mixed company, so it became relegated to groups of urban Blacks. It wasn't until the late 1960s and '70s that Black cinema (and Blaxploitation films) became popular, giving way to the colloquial speech used amongst Black Americans. Then, during the 1980s, the meteoric rise of hip hop further exemplified and showcased a differentiated use of language. Consequently, you had the term "nigga" being used in film and even more rampantly being sold on cassettes and CDs to millions of individuals all over the world. That brings us to little ol' me, sitting in front of my boom box with my headphones on, being exposed to a term on *The Chronic* that I had never previously heard referenced before. In retrospect, it all makes perfect sense, but even without the sociological knowledge as a child, my nine-year old brain was in the process of detonating. Very small pieces of growth at work.

16

Corporal punishment was real within the Louisiana state school system. And from my vantage point, the Black kids always got it a little bit worse than everyone else. If a student did something that was considered grossly out of line, the teacher had the authority to hit them with a ruler in the hallway outside of the classroom. It wasn't just one ruler either, but two of them taped together, and the reasons for being reprimanded were subjective. The litany of racial tragedies that had occurred in American history were extreme examples of the logic of America's ethnic caste system. I was looking at a microcosm of this system on a daily basis. The moral arrangements seemed completely out of whack, and it all trickled into the minds of the youth.

From a visual standpoint, consistently seeing Black students getting hit more often by their White teachers would liken itself to situations that were all too common from the past. There was too much room for personal bias to become a factor in the manner in which punishments were carried out. In one respect, I wish I could have stuck around longer to see how things progressed, but my desire to do this would have been from a sociological perspective. That would have been my curious side, searching for situations to analyze.

When my father and I would go for jogs at the local high school track, I'd often wonder what it was like for the teens who were beginning to date. Postbellum folklore is riddled with asinine social taboos. But as far as my own well-being, I'm glad that I was afforded the ability to get out. Having to go through puberty in such an environment would have probably taken quite a debilitating toll. Especially given the fact I wasn't born or bred in that area. My visceral feelings would have most likely led me to become obstinate to many of their social norms and possibly turn into a pariah.

Our next location would be Stafford, Virginia, where my family would live while my father worked at the Pentagon. Stafford definitely seemed like a quintessential spot to raise a family. It was rural but not country. In close proximity to major cities without being too urban. Low amounts of crime, decent schools, and very little poverty. If existing in Louisiana was an indoctrination to exist within a racist society, then life in Stafford was like a master's course on working around a prejudiced system. Louisiana brought you racism live and in color. There was never any beating around the bush. The racial intolerance in Northern Virginia was more like a slow-release drug. So very concealed. At the time, I would never have expected to face more covert bigotry by moving farther north. In mid-1990s Stafford, if you graduated with honors from the class on mild prejudice, your goal wasn't to learn how to win. It was more to become adept at the art of not losing. Winning meant playing the long game. It meant taking things in stride while consistently bettering yourself. It meant finding your own sense of independence by any means necessary. In 1994, Stafford was a true suburb. A long lost child of urban America. A causal effect of White flight.

My family moved to a neighborhood called St. George's Estates. The name sounds more regal than it actually was, although it was very nice. All of the homes had three stories including a basement. Safety was a major concern of my parents and St. George's offered that amenity. There wasn't much diversity (at the time, you weren't going to get diversity anywhere in Stafford), but a lot of the kids were around my age. At the very least, it meant there were always people to play with. Living there contributed to a lot of enjoyment, especially during snow storms or whenever my friends and I would have roller hockey tournaments. It was a cozy spot and pretty secure. A typical middle-class rural suburb. Maybe even "post-rural" if that's even a term. The environment was transitioning from being very country into becoming much more of a metropolitan offshoot of Interstate 95. I certainly couldn't complain.

17

Unlike the Deep South, where African Americans appeared to be plentiful, the northern region of the south was sparser in terms of its Black population density. Not knowing this as a ten-year-old, it left me shocked to see I was one of maybe four or five African American children in the entire fifth grade. Out of maybe one hundred students, we made up about 5 percent. It wasn't until after our Holiday Break that another Black student appeared in my class. The new kid was a Black girl, and my class-mates made endless humorous references to her skin color. "Oh look, now Justin can have a girlfriend." These eye-rolling jokes went on for weeks. My bitterness was increasing and becoming a normal emotion. I was never met with any violence, so I can't act like my experiences were synonymous with notable racist situa-tions from the past. I was, however, referred to as "Blackie" on a daily basis. When I'd play football at recess and we'd be picking teams, someone would always say, "we'll take 'Blackie.'" I was never called a "nigger" to my face, but the phrase was thrown around in my presence in an extremely cavalier manner. It was like the students didn't want to refer to most black people by their name, so "nigger" became the preferred adjective.

One of the most uncomfortable moments I recall came

during history class. For a child like myself, learning about history was always a source of inspiration. This harps back to the time I spent in Germany becoming exposed to the *Eyes On The Prize* documentary. Being educated about such heavy periods in American history at a very young age left me with a knowledge base that I really wanted to discuss with others. Ideally, I would have conversed on these matters with my Black peers (assuming they even existed), but it may have been too much for most to handle. I definitely avoided having these discussions with my parents, as I felt they would be jaded in their perspective. Honestly, I'm really glad I was made aware of such content. But then, in the fifth grade, came the unit on slavery, which was followed by the unit on Reconstruction. Next up was the section on the lynching era, and then the civil rights movement.

These are heavy topics in general, but imagine being met with sneers and giggles as the White students deflected from the serious nature by throwing their jokes back onto me. Honestly, I grew to despise Black History Month, as the pure nature of the subject matter left a massive bullseye on my head.

In one instance, a few of my acquaintances and I were sitting around discussing little bits and pieces about life, in whatever context that means to a ten-year-old. One of my friends mentioned how his father was getting caught up in a divorce case because he had been cheating on his wife. Randomly, he informed us that the woman in question happened to be Black. At that moment, another student proceeded to fake it as if he was throwing up in a disgusted reaction because the woman mentioned was African American. He wretched over and over and put on a show that was intended to imitate someone dying. The dude literally said, "Ewww, your dad fucked a Black woman?! That's disgusting and isn't right!!" I sat there in awe of the monumental amount of ignorance in my presence. The look on my face must have been rampant with disgust and bewilderment. I didn't vocalize any distaste, but my displeasure at his perspective was obvious. Following these remarks, the student went on an inarticulate rant about how the South would rise again. This was equally as disgusting as his opinion on the Black woman. I had been recently removed from the Deep South, and for someone to feel as though that perspective would "rise again" sounded both cold-hearted and offensive. Who in the hell would want the conditions of the "old South" to rise again? One would have to be living in an unconscious bubble to embrace that ideology. I mean, I suppose a White supremacist would find it appealing. But it really wasn't *him*, the student, speaking. He was the mouthpiece for those who had cultured him. The whole thing was unfortunate but very real. I was surrounded by evil viewpoints that were readily nurturing children.

People can feel all kinds of illogical and preposterous ways about other humans, but this child really was under the impression that an entire region was going to become reestablished to some form of antebellum grandeur. Like some type of modern-day Southern insurgency. Given what I assumed about this kid's intelligence level, I don't think he knew very much about the old South other than what his backwoods parents had trained him to think. I know my assertion sounds judgmental, but that's how I felt. It was as if he was living in a fabled late-19th-century trance. Some perverse variety of *Gone with the Wind* (which is problematic within itself). I have no idea if his goal was to connect his points with his youthful depiction of bigotry. Clearly his level of obliviousness was peaking, but that was par for the course with this guy.

As time progressed, I became so frustrated that I started faking sick to alleviate the bombardment of ludicrous comments and critiques. My tactics were fairly simple. I'd wake up before everyone else and then shove the back end of a pencil down my throat until I puked. In addition to it being uncomfortable, it was also fairly painful. So I also had that working in my favor, in terms of appearing to be aching. I'd present the "throw up" to my mother, which would force her to let me stay home. I only did this two or three times, but those days off really helped. The whole process felt like searching for Black dignity within a White world, even if gaining that dignity meant hiding from reality. You had to consistently prove you were "better than." But better than what? Better than the average White person? Simple attacks based on skin color and erroneous perceptions were all around. The aggressions were very micro, but they chipped away at my overall well-being on a regular basis. Actions had to be taken to negate what was being lost.

Slowly but surely, the ridicule subsided. Things did get easier, but in hindsight, maybe I just got used to the general customs of the area. In addition to being the only Black kid in my class, I was also one of the only ones who hadn't lived their entire life in a mostly rural environment. It was just like how I hadn't been brought up in Louisiana, and therefore wasn't immersed in their "traditions." A lot of my White peers were born and bred in the backwoods. They weren't literally from the backwoods, but I'm just using the term to denote the fact they knew nothing other than living in a non-urban center or "the sticks."

I was probably the only African American some of these people had ever been around on a regular basis. Unlike in Germany, where existing as an anomaly led to being praised or treated like a glorified pet, being the outlier in Virginia led to mistreatment, misjudgment, and misinterpretation. With that being said, a major factor in the reduction of the bullying was due to the fact I didn't fit into their stereotypes at all. To them, I was supposed to speak poorly, appear unkempt, keep quiet, and underperform academically. In reality, most of what I embodied went against their grain. I outdid most of them in the classroom, had a fairly confident disposition (despite my circumstances), dressed well, and spoke with appropriate grammar. I also had better writing skills than the majority of them, so my English assignments consistently came back with higher marks. Things were the same when it came to math. Some of the bullies were starting to feel a tad inferior, and most of them shut up. I never received any apologies, but actions began to shift. In fact, throughout all of this, the most offensive attitude projected in my direction was the notion, "*You're* ok, but . . ." It was as if being around me, as a perceived outlier, was alright, but if too many people who looked similar came around, there would be some issues. That perspective really threw my mind into a tizzy. Like being in the Bizarro World. As difficult as it was to comprehend, my minor successes were boosting my confidence. Did I begin to behave in more of a pompous manner? Hell yeah, I did.

Over the next few months, it became my turn to do the tormenting, which I took no shame in. I don't think my reactions accounted for anything very serious. Just some laughing at test scores. Being extra excited when the teacher handed out report cards (as it gave me the opportunity to degrade others). Maybe a few snarky remarks if a student showed up in a pair of PRO-Keds, as opposed to some Jordans or fresh Reeboks. LA Gears or Pumas would have even been acceptable, I guess. My snobbish streak was really showing. By no means was this the right way to behave, but I honestly didn't give a fuck. This is my biased opinion on the situation. In my head, I felt like my responses were warranted. The only thing I was worried about was being ganged up on. Lucky for me, I was never met with such a fate. Once general respect was earned, a lot of the turmoil began to soften. I guess some of my old villainous traits were showing, but these were *my* reactions to *their* behavior, which I deemed gross. Maybe my moral compass was skewed, but I wasn't going to be backed into a corner without some type of fight.

The end of my stint as a fifth grader in Stafford culminated with my father sending me off to a summer football camp. I had played a little bit in a local recreational league and performed pretty well. Personally, I thought I was fairly good, but I was just comparing myself to the others in my bubble. The camp was sponsored by the great Washington Redskins' receiver, Art Monk. I didn't really want to go, but my dad convinced me it was the right thing to do. Terry really hyped the whole thing up. I would have much preferred to spend my summer relaxing and doing a lot of nothing. I had never been to a summer camp, but if I *was* going to go, this type seemed like a perfect fit. All sports and socialization with male peers. Plus, it was only a week taken out of my summer schedule. But in all honesty, it was anything but perfection.

The facility was full of many of the best players on the East Coast, and I ended up feeling so inadequate that it completely dejected me from wanting to continue playing the sport. I knew I was an okay player, but I was too small and didn't have enough drive to become elite. A lot of the other attendees appeared to care so much more about bettering their athletic skill sets than I did. They were hyper focused on improving their craft. My time at the camp wasn't enjoyable in the least, but it was definitely helpful in terms of me realizing what I DIDN'T want to pursue. I guess that kind of realization is virtuous in itself. In that general moment, I left football behind and started to focus much more on tennis. With all of this being said, one aspect from camp really stuck with me in terms of its lasting prominence. I would often complain about the daily activities to my roommate throughout the week. His response was always, "Ya know, Marlowe, life sucks and then you die." I guess it could have been a slight nod to the Nas track "Life's A Bitch," where the rapper AZ says, "life's a bitch and then you die." That phrase has lived rent free in my head ever since. I'm not going to say that I love it, because it comes off as slightly morbid and cynical, but I do appreciate it for its general candor. Given all that I was going through at the time, it made me feel some type of way, and you can take whatever you want from that. I didn't feel like having a slightly bleak outlook was inherently negative.

18

Making the journey from elementary into middle school had its peaks and valleys. This would be the case for anyone dealing with such a rite of passage, but I suppose there are levels to it all. A positive that came with living in Northern Virginia during these times was that it was becoming increasingly diverse. Being in close proximity to the Pentagon and the Quantico Marine Base meant military families were arriving in high numbers. Stafford wouldn't have been considered as part of the Northern Virginia locale, but it is now. Actually, it might have technically lay within Northern Virginia but residents didn't associate it with the area. Being inundated with varying cultures was comforting. It was nice to see people of color in the neighborhood. It was certainly reassuring to not be the only Black child in a classroom any longer. Not to imply that color is everything, but when color divides the mind, it seems to have a magnified effect on so much else.

While much was being altered in terms of the student body, much less could be said for the ones doing the educating. Every single one of my teachers was White, except for a lone African American man who taught wood shop. I don't really know if this ethnic disparity had a major impact on myself or any of my peers, but I know it was very one sided from an optics perspective. Honestly, in those days I completely expected my teachers to be White. And this is coming from an individual whose mother was a Black teacher. I considered her to be an outlier. What does it do to a child to see all of his or her teachers being from one general racial background? In the moment, one may not feel any significant impact, but the lasting effects can permeate the mind. More importantly, they can permeate the heart and really fuck with your self-esteem.

These are the people students look up to on a daily basis. The ones we get some of our most pertinent information from. The ones we trust. And if we never see a diverse representation, how can the students who watch from the sidelines ever intrinsically feel like we can do what they do in large numbers? Think about how difficult it must be for an African American child to legitimately think he or she can become president. Even though it's been done, it's still one out of forty-six. Roughly 98 percent of American presidents have been White, heterosexual men. Zero percent have been women and 0 percent have been openly a part of the LGBTQ+ community. We've had one Native American vice president, Charles Curtis, who served under Herbert Hoover in 1929, and most are aware of current Vice President Kamala Harris's status as a member of multiple marginalized ethnic groups. What does this convey to other minority groups who legally inhabit this nation? That may not matter in terms of what I'm about to say, but it DEFINITELY references the power and weight our teachers hold.

One day, I made an off-the-cuff comment about a young lady. Her name was Christina, and she always wore super short shorts. This was how I knew her at the time; the girl in the hot pants. Well, I knew her for other reasons, but none that are significant here. Her shorts were some of the shortest that I had ever seen up until then. Not quite Daisy Dukes but close to it. Honestly, I don't know how she never got a dress code violation, but I guess I'm glad she didn't. Clearly I'm being sarcastic.

Our English class used to occasionally read poetry outside in the school courtyard. The heat would often become blistering, and Christina's shorts used to stick to her skin. It was due to the sweat, but this didn't cause me to notice any less. She was a pale-skinned blonde girl. She had a slender figure and a gregarious personality. None of this mattered to me in the least, in terms of what I was viewing on those days. It was all about the pants, which were usually white. Almost like a bleached white. Because of their extremely light color, when she would sweat, the garments took on a see-through quality. Identifiably translucent. This would happen day after day, and at one point, I made a reference to what I'd been seeing. During a class lecture in the library, I told a friend, "In those shorts, Christina's ass looks like a juicy orange." The comment was lighthearted. It was simply a critique laced in comparative sarcasm.

Either way, the comment made its way through our little circle of friends. And then our teachers somehow got wind of it. This meant people had been talking a lot about something that shouldn't have had any legs. At least, not in my opinion. I guess I underestimated the interests of sixth graders. Regardless, someone felt the need to tell my math teacher, and she felt the need to call me into the hallway to have a discussion.

Mrs. Blecha (pronounced Bleck-ah). I'll never forget her name. Her anger was seething and projecting toward me because of what she heard I had said. Her vitriol was emitting from her pores. I didn't entirely understand why, but it was. If she could have hit me, I think she would have. She told me my words were so offensive and would be considered sexual harassment in a court of law. I'm pretty sure she was lying (or maybe just ignorantly informed), but upon hearing this, I was devastated. I'd never commit such a crime. Certainly not knowingly. I mean, I was a twelve-year-old who had made a silly joke. I didn't even think I had committed any wrongdoing at all. I simply gave a loose opinion about a girl's body to a third party. If I had said it to Christina, it would have been a completely different story; but I didn't.

I wanted to fight back, but I wasn't sure if it was a sixth grader's place to do so. Mrs. Blecha's bitterness didn't appear genuine at all. It gave the impression it was derived from a place riddled with bias. Not only did she look like someone who had walked right out of 1880, but she acted like it as well. Maybe to her I had stepped out of my place, which caused her to seemingly fabricate the seriousness of my actions. I'm in no way implying that what I said was completely okay, but telling a twelve-year-old that he had committed sexual harassment on a whim was irresponsible and outlandish in my mind. She hadn't delved into the specifications of what had been said. She didn't even hear anything first-hand nor was she privy to an audio copy. She didn't have a law degree and appeared to be using this tactic to play on my youthful unawareness. This was the first and only time I can recall ever actually expressing any somberness during a school day.

Upon walking back to my desk, I was devastated at being accused of sexual misconduct. So much so that I couldn't hold back my tears. Had I done something evil? Had my mildly callous nature led me to make a threatening comment about this young lady? I really didn't think it was too serious, which could have been completely my problem. Maybe what I had done would be classified as sexual impropriety. If the young lady had gotten wind of my words and felt harassed, then I definitely would have been at fault, albeit unknowingly. Wouldn't a better course of action have been to advise me not to speak in such a fashion out loud, in the future? I wished that my comments had stayed between my friend and me. Maybe I was naive to believe such a thing would be the case in middle school. Anyhow, my emotions spilled over. Mrs. Blecha didn't seem to care and went ahead and passed out our most recently graded math exam. Coincidentally, I received the highest grade in the class, and with my head laid flat against the table, my tears completely drenched the paper. To me, the accusation was so absurd I didn't care if anyone saw me in that somber state. Once again, I could be wrong, but I couldn't figure out any other reason why she would have been so upset. After all, in this situation I had complete plausible deniability. I could have just said that I didn't utter those words. It was all a bunch of hearsay. Obviously I'm admitting that I said them, but it was my teacher's fury intertwined with her shaming verbiage that made me so uncomfortable. Ultimately, my punishment was to have one of my parents sign a notice confirming they were aware of what I had said. In reality, there was NO WAY I was going to bring such a claim to them, so I forged it and then brought it back to school "signed." Hell, I guess forgery was the *real* crime.

19

In addition to social bullshit constantly flaring up, my artistic side was beginning to flourish, and I decided to join the band. I think we had the option to choose band, drama, or chorus. There may have been an alternative elective, but it eludes me at the moment. I was leery at first, as I hadn't had any experience playing a musical instrument other than the recorder in elementary school. Of course, everybody had to play the recorder in elementary school, and it seemed pretty lame. It was so squeaky and cheap sounding. The students never treated them with any significant respect. Plus, everyone had to play in unison, which ended up sounding like extreme overkill, compounded with the fact most of the kids sounded shitty as hell.

Being a band member offered up a completely fresh feeling. It carried with it a bit of an isolating sensibility, which was kind of cool in its own right. We got to carry our little bags around school with our instruments in them. The band crew would engage in conversations filled with jargon and gossip that other kids weren't privy to. There were band romances, which I'm sure doesn't come as a surprise. Other than occasionally being referred to as a band geek, it was a pretty sweet gig. Much like with sports, one's success was totally merit based.

I was a part of the percussion team, which had its own class. If I remember correctly, the idea was for the percussion group to practice separately from the concert band, and then join forces once we'd reached a certain skill level. My percussion teacher, Mrs. Sutherland, taught the students how to read music, carry out rudiments, and analyze meter and rhythm. Percussion carries with it a multitude of instruments, so the intent was for us to become well versed in them all: the cowbell, drums, triangle, cymbals, wood block, brushes, and the xylophone. The latter was my absolute favorite and where I stood out. After about a month, it became clear I was the best xylophone player in the bunch. It was also where Mrs. Sutherland advised me to place my focus. When we moved into playing with the concert band, the others handled the overall percussion duties and I handled all of the melodic parts via the xylophone, or the mallets, as they would often be called.

The concert band director's name was Mrs. Mandoudis, and she was absolutely fierce, demanding, and professional. Not in a tyrannical sense, but more like a powerful maternal teddy bear. She also seemed to be a bit overqualified, as she could have easily directed a high school or college band. Mrs. Mandoudis always commanded respect and never really played around outside of some occasional off-the-cuff sarcastic banter. Conversely, she did her best to make sure we didn't fuck around either. She always expected a lot from her students and gave so much of herself. She got the best out of us as young musicians. I really do think a part of her demeanor rubbed off on me, as she was the first teacher I revered. While I was the only xylophone player, I always felt like she held me in a high regard. I could totally be wrong, but I felt that way at the time. She pushed me to do my best and simultaneously showed me she cared.

The most fruitful aspect of being in the band was the fact it was a very diverse conglomerate of kids. Of course it was mostly White, but there was a solid mix of Blacks, Asians, and Hispanics. It also seemed like a place that cultivated a decent amount of diversity of thought. We were all a little different but had to come together with the common purpose of performing well as a unit. I'll never forget some of the interactions I had with my fellow percussionists; Anthony, Justin, Chris, Seth and myself had so much fun goofing off before and after class (never during). I would laugh uncontrollably at times. Those guys were hilarious. I'm actually surprised we got away with the shit we did, and I was the goody two-shoes of the bunch. Definitely the least likely to act out but occasionally I exhibited a rebellious streak. Not like the others, but I was showing out in my own way.

Middle school was such a tough time and I was slowly learning more about myself. Little bits and pieces were coming together. Life is like one massive puzzle, and for me, playing in the band was a miniscule piece in the grand scheme of it all. You're trying your best to stand out, all while blending in at the same time. I could tell sections of my emergent self were forming. Budding like a flower that was taking far too long to blossom, but blossoming nonetheless. As stressful as it was, it was also super entertaining. You get to learn so much about your skill sets and those possessed by others. Teamwork is integral, so it's important to be selfless. We got to travel all over the county and perform at different venues. Sometimes we interacted with the students from other schools. We even took a field trip to Washington, DC, as a part of a field trip to see a professional orchestra.

Other than visiting my grandparents, I didn't visit DC very often. Although I was born there, I knew very little about the area as a whole. I couldn't tell you the difference between the varying sections of the city, nor could I recognize prominent street names (other than Pennsylvania Avenue or M Street). I was pumped to go and was certainly looking forward to getting out of school for the day.

We took a charter bus, which I loved riding because I got to bring my Walkman. It gave me the chance to isolate myself within my little music world. I guess the type of bus wouldn't have made a difference, but charter buses just offered more comfort. It was akin to being at recess back on the playground in Louisiana. The days when I'd opt not to play football and just walk the perimeter grounds analyzing music. There was a little bit of anxiety that came with trying to find a seat or someone to sit next to. If you had a crush on someone, you'd want to sit by them but could easily be too afraid to ask. If you did have the balls to ask and everything went as planned, you'd still have to deal with other students gossiping about it. It was all a part of the game. Confidence, fear, apprehension, bravado, and gumption all wound together. But the way it all manifested was very interesting. None of us really knew what we were doing. I suppose it's all par for the course during one's middle-school years.

We arrived in the city and everything went accordingly. Our class saw the concert during the early afternoon and then we were given the opportunity to walk the city and get some lunch. There were tight restrictions on where we could go and we had a buddy system to ensure we each had another student with us at all times. Somehow I was able to convince my buddy I was going to get a sandwich and that I'd be fine by myself. I didn't even have a clue where I was going. I just walked aimlessly until I stumbled upon an appealing place to get an Italian sub. Well, I did end up finding one, but it was way outside of the jurisdiction that Mrs. Mandoudis had legislated. I paid for my sandwich and then left the shop, trying to look cool. I pretended I knew where I was and the direction I was heading. In reality, I was clueless. Twelve years old and totally unaware of my surroundings. I could have easily been twenty-five blocks away from my crew AND I was on a time crunch in order to avoid being left behind. I didn't think they would actually leave me, but my nerves were on edge. I hadn't even made a point to mentally catalog any landmarks which could help lead me back to safety. I was literally just walking, hoping I was heading in the right direction but really having no idea.

Panic started to set in. My heart rate was peaking and I was beginning to sweat profusely. For the first time in my life, I was really worried about what could happen to me. This wasn't like when I was concerned about losing my action figures on the plane heading home from Germany. My personal safety was at risk. My brain was in worst-case-scenario mode. What if I get abducted? What if my anxiety peaks and I get hit by a car? How would I respond if I were robbed or held at gunpoint? I wasn't from the streets or "about that life." Was I going to end up like one of those missing children on the side of milk cartons? I began to think about my parents and how they would view what had happened. In that one instance, I just wanted to be back home with my family. Despite the nuances I was dealing with and the imperfections in my life, I was actually a fairly privileged little kid. A privileged kid who was lost in the middle of Washington, DC, and missing his parents. My solution was to continue walking. Something inside told me if I just kept walking, I'd notice a building or a sign that would clue me in. Right then, hearing Mrs. Mandoudis's voice would have been music to my ears (no pun intended). I rushed from block to block at a brisk pace; wanting to run, but thinking that if I did so, I'd look a bit ridiculous. As frightened as I was, I didn't want to look like "that kid." A young Black boy sprinting through the streets of DC searching for his class. Clearly, if I had acted as such, it would have made perfect sense, but I wasn't willing to go there just yet. So, the quick-paced walking ensued.

By this point, the sweat was pouring down my face and beginning to soak my shirt. I waited at a stoplight, crossed the street, and then made an immediate left turn onto the next block. It was right then when I saw our charter bus. My heart dropped and relief set in. Of course, Mrs. Mandoudis charged at me as if she was infuriated but then gave me a big hug. I knew she was just glad I was safe. The entire episode had been my fault. A case of me doing too much, but I had made it back in one piece. Everything was okay, and I was ecstatic to be going home. Although I was the one in the wrong, I felt a sense of pride in the fact I had overcome this little piece of self-inflicted adversity. I was the villain in terms of my actions but internalized a little bit of heroism at the same time. I was glad to be back around my friends and couldn't get back to Stafford soon enough.

My time as a member of the band was awesome and constructive in terms of what it added to my life but ultimately it was short lived. The attention I began to give to athletics really started to take over. With academic rigors increasing, I didn't have enough time to allocate to school, sports, and the band. Something had to get cut, and it was going to have to be the music. Maybe some of this was me trying to appease my father, as he was very much invested in sports, but I'd be lying if I said I wasn't passionate about tennis as well. It's unfortunate, because I was a talented xylophone player, but as one matures, the dedication to practice time needs to increase exponentially. This wasn't something I was willing to take on, but my time in the band really increased my overall development. I was able to gain insights into my abilities and see that I could have success at just about anything that I put my mind to when I really cared.

20

While living in Virginia exposed me to more of an "ethnic variety" in the classroom, it also led to more intense exposure to adult Black women. This was a first for me. Other than my mother, who always seemed to be at a distance emotionally, yet adjacent to me in terms of proximity, I hadn't really been exposed to many African American ladies. Now, I was regularly in the presence of both sets of aunts, grandmothers, and cousins. The majority of my immediate family members were from the DMV (DC, Maryland, and Virginia) area, so moving to Stafford brought me closer to them. As much as it was positive in terms of exposure, it still created some significant division.

My mother's side of the family was well educated, established, and socially conservative. Never getting too wild or behaving in a manner that might be considered uncouth. My aunt Lisa (my mother's sister) was sharp and eccentric. A quirky individual with a real zest for life. Very strong in math and science, specifically. She graduated from the prestigious Brown University, an Ivy League institution. Lisa's sense of family always stood out to me as being a notable quality. She also embodied a sense of stringency when it came to issues she felt strongly about. Her, my mother, and grandmother were all old-fashioned

Christians in a typical sense. They each attempted to indoctrinate their families with this perspective, which didn't go over so well with me.

My grandmother, Helen, was a very stern woman with a good heart and a lot of flair. Fashionable and never one to turn down the opportunity to tell a long-winded story about her life experiences. When she'd get angry at her grandkids, she would sometimes put a ruler to our knuckles. It didn't hurt much, but the overall execution seemed harsh. It seemed antiquated to me, but we had to accept it for what it was. Helen had the gift of gab and an infectious laugh. Her disposition was akin to Rose from *The Golden Girls*, although she wasn't remotely scatterbrained. Being that she was from southern Virginia, she had dealt with a lot of racism and was not shy about sharing these trials with others. I don't know if she actually harbored any animosity toward White people, but at times her verbiage seemed as though she did. She may have just had her guard up because of certain life experiences, but she definitely wasn't going to treat someone unfairly because of their skin color. Like I've said, she was religious as hell, but I can honestly say that Helen really did believe in her heart everything the Bible teaches. Her faith was one of the only entities she would never waiver on.

My religious questioning would flare up from time to time but wouldn't become concerning to others until later. The notion of adhering to the words of the Bible were far more successful with my aunt's family, which would still imply my grandmother did a good job instituting said principles into her daughters. Lisa bore two children, Allison and Cameron, who are both phenomenal individuals in their own right. Both are extremely intelligent and appear to rarely upset the apple cart. They grew up to have loving partners and became engaged in fruitful careers. The maternal side of my family were all avid participants in the Washington-area Black Baptist community. Financially secure and walking a straight and narrow line.

My father's side was a bit more discombobulated and clearly

victims of White flight. With that being said, they are all loving people with huge hearts. Each and every one of them. Their general lack of higher education pushed them deeper into an already-marginalized demographic. As an adult, I know them to be held in high academic esteem, but as a child I didn't feel that way. They lived life in a much freer manner than what I had been exposed to. I never noticed any strict adherence to religious faith, on the surface (which I didn't see as a bad thing at all). One major commonality was that they all possessed a certain amount of strength and independence. Their primary divide was, socially, they were on opposite ends of almost every aspect of life in comparison to my mother's side. Still, it was important for me to be around them, as it broadened my circle of influence. Although I didn't spend nearly as much time in the presence of the women as I did the men in my family, the differences between both sides let me know that I stood in a tense place. Clearly this is a theme. It is one that was, is, and always will be a staple in my life.

I never got to know my grandfather on my dad's side. If my memory serves me correctly, I was only in his presence on two occasions. Once he split with my father's mother, he moved somewhere out west and started a completely new family of his own. I do, however, have lots of memories of my paternal grandma, Marguerite Lane, or Grandma Lane as we called her. She was a feisty motherfucker. I always thought something about her reminded me of the character Dorothy from *The Golden Girls*. Warmhearted but slightly truculent. Sometimes she even came off as kind of mean, which was never really the case. She just possessed a keen streak of determination and fortitude. A petite woman but very tough. Marguerite was always fun to be around, unless something was frustrating her. Usually, one could just wait out whatever was bothersome and she'd be fine. Her home was festive. My uncle Maurice used to refer to it as the "fun house." The total antithesis of Helen's place. She loved to cook. Whenever my family would visit for Thanksgiving, the aroma in her kitchen would be so robust. The scent of traditional dishes intertwined with some preferred soul food was almost stifling. I'll never forget it. Her generosity was glaring. Every Christmas, my siblings and I could usually count on receiving at least $200 from her. Being an older single woman really led her to develop an intense amount of toughness. She would always pretend like if one of her grandkids acted out, she would spank us or use some other type of force to get us in line. Marguerite was too loving for that, although the threat was intimidating. Her old-school personality showed up a lot. She had a thick exterior but was a complete softie on the inside. I never got very close with her, but I can say that she was always enjoyable to be around.

21

The Black men around me were all amazing sources of triumph, which was truly important for me to witness during adolescence. I'd hoped to be such a symbol to others as I grew older. My father, Uncle Maurice, and both of my grandfathers were prodigious humans with multiple nuances that differentiated themselves from one another. Some were equipped with more practical skills while others possessed a certain flare, which lent itself to their unique spirit. They were each flawed in their own right, but that didn't inhibit their influential nature. All humans have drawbacks, which can be exasperated by the realities one experiences. Seeing intelligent, articulate, financially stable Black men before me was paramount to so many of my other points of guidance. Each of them had overcome much adversity, whether it be social, economic, or interfamilial. Maybe even all three. A blueprint was being provided, even if I had no interest in following it. I was too young to engage in detailed discussions with them, but their pixie dust graced me. Sometimes I didn't like what I heard. Sometimes they sounded jaded. On other occasions I was confused. But most of the time I felt inspired. Visiting with them more often provided me with so much game. The type that still resonates with me currently.

My father's knowledge base typically projected when he'd speak about sports, as I've previously mentioned with respect to our bond. His personality would reverberate in such moments. Almost like he couldn't wait to feed you with information. When he and I would discuss some of the football clips I'd watch after school, it was almost as if he was there with the athletes. Maybe living vicariously through those who had athletically made it a little further than him.

Stories about Tony Dorsett always stood out. The supreme greatness of Walter Payton was a staple. Joe Montana, Warren Moon, and Johnny Unitas were all masters of the quarterback position. Bo Jackson, Deion Sanders, and Steve Largent were mentioned as individuals with phenomenal athletic prowess. He loved to talk about important games. The Ice Bowl. The first two Super Bowls. The infamous title showdown in 1969 between the New York Jets and the Baltimore Colts, when Joe Namath boldly predicted a Jets victory.

Once my interests began to include tennis, he provided verbal context when talking about Ilie Nastase, John McEnroe, Martina Navratilova, Jimmy Connors, Pete Sampras, Arthur Ashe, and Andre Agassi. He emphasized Navratilova's fitness regimen, as she transcended the sport with her commitment to muscular and cardiovascular development. Watching Andre play live was the first time I knew I wasn't going to be able to pursue a professional tennis career. Seeing his elite ball-striking ability firsthand was enough to push me into a shell. It was becoming obvious to me that my skills were pretty far behind the curve. Nonetheless, because sports were important to me as a kid, my father's influence was considerable. In hindsight, maybe I should have asked him more questions about life outside of sports. Dug a little deeper into the notions of why he turned out as he did. Questions about his childhood and the relationships he had with his family. Instead, we both stayed in our respective comfort zones.

Although I never really delved into this as a child, in retrospect, my dad was actually a pretty fly dude back in his day. Maybe this contributed to where I get a bit of my stylistic influence from, which isn't to sound like I'm tooting my own horn or anything. During the early and mid-1980s, Terry used to routinely rock fresh Reebok or Nike shoes, Adidas tracksuits, polos by Sergio Tacchini, Lacoste, and Le Tigre. Hell, these are all brands that I currently adore. He drove a fresh-looking little Saab hatchback and always kept it spotless. During the '90s, he always had the latest pair of sneakers on hand, even if he actually wore them when participating in athletic activities. This would seem like sacrilege in today's sneakerhead culture, but back then I guess it was commonplace. I distinctly recall him being fond of the Nike Air Max series, specifically the classic Air Max 95s. The green, gray, and black colorway was his favorite. He'd usually wear them in tandem with a pair of knee-high socks. Back then, I thought the choice was a bit dated and lame, but in hindsight, it really added to his entire aesthetic. He even used to unapologetically don a fluorescent fanny pack. During that era, it might have seemed like a questionable style choice for a heterosexual Black man, but now it would be considered pretty stylish. After some re-examination, perspectives can really change with time. His style said a lot about who he was as a man, as it should. He pulled his fits off pretty well, and I give him major props for that.

My uncle, Maurice (Lisa's husband), was like a steel trap when it came to music, which always helped put us on the same accord. Other than myself and a few others, it's been rare to encounter someone who found it appealing to openly hold a conversation about popular music in its general entirety. My dad could do it some, but Maurice's knowledge base was broader. Like his wife, he was a graduate of Brown University. His mind was always seeking to explore new terrain; to gain insights into uncharted territory. As a child, I used to rummage through his record collection just to peek at the album covers. It was enthralling. The Average White Band, Parliament, The

Jacksons, ABBA, Ray Parker Jr., and Chaka Khan, just to name a few. I loved it. Just looking at the album art was so thought provoking. That kind of attention to detail is something kids today will never get to experience (unless they delve into the older stuff, obviously). Back then, you got to see the cover, backing, and the inside liner notes. Each of these would provide its own unique take on the project. And all of them were important in their own right. Maurice was a one-of-a-kind type of guy, and I've always appreciated his involvement in my life.

His spirits were typically high, even when they were low. Much like my father, he had an affinity for sharing and discussing topics he was well-versed in. He, too, was a sports enthusiast who knew so much about football, tennis, and basketball. Maurice was also pretty up to speed on social and political topics. Just as easily as he could hold a conversation about the NFL's leading rusher, he was able to discuss whatever the latest rumblings were in pop culture circles. His personality reminded me of one of the "cool guys" in a Blaxploitation film. Maybe a bit like Shaft but in a more universal sense. Outgoing but relaxed. Gregarious, but not to the point of being annoying. Certainly, an irreplaceable type of dude.

Both of my grandfathers were symbols of Black success during an era when that was seen as a rarity and a threat to White supremacy. It was the 1950s, when most African Americans (especially in the South) were still living beneath the steel-toed boot of Jim Crow. My biological grandfather's name was Leon, and my step-grandfather's name was Winston. Both on my mother's side. Leon and my grandmother, Helen, divorced in the early 1960s and then she remarried to Winston. Both were educators. Leon was as resourceful as they come. He knew cars like the back of his hand and could fix almost anything. Very stern, no nonsense, and supremely authentic. He was also an avid outdoorsman. Loved to hunt, fish, and be close to the water. An "overalls and T-shirt" kind of man. One of the most identifiable aspects of his home was that he kept a deer head mounted on his wall, above his TV set.

My family used to visit him in Wilmington, Delaware, a few times per year. He never remarried, and he and I weren't very close, but I could tell my mother was extremely fond of him. I never knew a whole lot about his personal tastes in anything artistic, but during one of our visits to his home, something specific sparked some curiosity. His house wasn't particularly large, and the rooms were fairly small. A rustic spot with a cozy feeling. Nothing that I was remotely familiar with. He had a nice basement with a fancy pool table. It was dusty but fancy nonetheless. There were three rooms in his home that were equipped with tape players connected to a speaker system that could play throughout the house. In each of these rooms, he had the Michael Jackson *Thriller* tape on deck. This meant that he had purchased the same album three times so that it could be played in each of those rooms by whoever was occupying the area at a given time. The fact he had *Thriller* on deck in multiple rooms always stood out to me as being kind of wild. It really solidified the cultural impact of that record for me and contributed to a tidbit of intuition into my grandpa. I probably should have asked some questions back then, because I was certainly intrigued. It could have been a critical bonding moment for us. Lost moments in the abyss of time but a slight learning experience for sure. The more we know about our relatives, the better we can cling to bits and pieces of our own existence.

Winston was much more of a white-collar man. Very genuine and always dressed with a conservative sartorial aesthetic: button-up shirts and a tailored pair of slacks. His shirts were typically tucked in. Polished loafers. He and my grandmother were devout Christians, maybe even to a fault. Neither of them ever budged on their literal interpretation of the Bible. At least not that I can recall. I don't know this to be factual, but they'd probably even tell you Jesus was a blond-haired, blue-eyed White man. Winston didn't say much, but when he did speak, it was usually something of merit. Wisdom was a keen trait of his, as well as his love for laughter, good candy, food, and educational discussions. He was a very loyal guy. Just like with Leon, I wish I had asked more questions about so many topics: his upbringing, religion, his experience as an educator, etc. I suppose that's a pervasive regret of mine. With that being said, becoming surrounded by these types of men during the early to mid-1990s provided me with a solid circle of guidance, even if it wasn't *always* immaculate.

During the weekends, my family would often make the drive from Stafford up to the DC/Maryland area to visit with both sides of the family. We'd usually hit Prince George's County, Maryland, first and then skip across town to Washington. This was fairly easy, as the areas were roughly a half hour from one another. My father's side always seemed to be turning up while my mother's side was turning down. One of my fondest memories with them was when my dad's half-sister, Shawn, took me for a ride in her Mustang 5.0. I think it was the same model that was referenced in Vanilla Ice's hit song "Ice Ice Baby." All that she really did was drive particularly fast around her neighborhood. Maybe to do a bit of showboating but also to have a moment with her nephew. Nothing super special, but to me it was exhilarating. My dad's family was steeped in urban culture while my mother's was far more demure (almost like a suburban African American family from the 1970s).

Per usual, my brother, sister, and I were caught in the middle. Sitting in between these two Black subcultures. I always thought that my father's side looked at us as being a bit prim and proper. Although we were clearly Black, I felt like we were viewed as being more polished than the average African American. It wasn't something that was ever said to me personally, but the vibes were effervescent. I can't speak on whether or not these attitudes were shared with either of my siblings. It wasn't easy, but the fact that these possible outlooks were coming from family made the discomfort more comforting. Things were easier to brush off or dismiss when it came to family. Maybe my feelings regarding their viewpoints were based on some of my own insecurities. So much of what life had presented me with was puzzling anyway. As my maturity escalated, I was beginning to understand *why* certain Black stereotypes existed, but internally it seemed asinine for people to project them as fact. It was like the human condition was far more basic than I had wanted to give it credit for. I was quickly learning that not everyone thought like me.

22

Intriguing elements to these changing demographics were engulfing me, but there was one I didn't see coming at all. As more African Americans populated the area, one would think my overall comfort level would increase simply because there were more black and brown faces. More kids who might have shared similar experiences and perspectives. More tolerance for situations uniquely affected by the "Black experience." I was more physically comfortable because the numbers made me stand out less. It was really nice to be around higher numbers of African Americans from a similar socioeconomic background. But ironically, things turned out to be tougher than expected.

Much like being caught between opposite ends of my family, the influx of Blacks into the area led to an emergence of two different types of Black people, as I saw it at the time. I say two types because that's how it would seem to a typical onlooker. The average person would see, on one side, African Americans who fit into their general stereotype. The type who wore their Blackness on their sleeve. Those who were boisterous about their preference to surround themselves with other Black people. Those who mainly listened to urban music and dressed in a manner that appealed to typical urban sensibilities.

On the other side, they'd see another incarnation of African Americans who were the antithesis to the aforementioned typecast. Those whose aesthetic appeared to be *trying* to fit into what conservative Whites would find acceptable. Clean cut and not remotely offensive. Nothing that aligned itself with counterculture. The kind who would rebuke hip hop, especially the burgeoning subgenre of gangsta rap. The type who would go out of their way to align themselves with Whites and be unapologetic about it. In some cases, even cozying up to "good ol' boy" types. In the mind of someone with this agenda, receiving the acceptance of the "good ol' boys" was like a badge of honor. Like being a member of an exclusive club of Blacks who transcended their skin color and were seen almost as White. The typical "token." I can even recall certain Black friends of mine being proud to refer to themselves as the "Whitest Black person in the room." Now, as I stated, I felt like the average person saw these two polar archetypes, but I began to feel as though a third existed, which I thought to be far more rare. They were rarer in terms of the individuals I was around at the given time. In reality, my assessment was completely incorrect. As I've grown, I can see this particular type was, and is, the most prevalent embodiment of the ethnic group, as it speaks to the overall diversity among us.

This third type didn't fit into either of the previous narratives, as it embraced qualities of so much without intently trying to embrace anything that wasn't natural. To be more specific, it took in what it was exposed to and used it for the betterment of the individual. It referenced a person who was comfortable enough in their own skin to go against the grain and dress/behave in a manner that appealed to them, all while knowing how to read a room in terms of its situational appropriateness. It could also apply to one who goes far left of center, if that is what would have mostly benefited them. Artistic tastes were a direct result of how they were cultured, rather than an attempt at pandering to a specific audience. Maybe even being a complete "square" but owning that moniker. Flying their proverbial flag proudly (in terms of whatever that would mean to them). One who, in some senses, could have a very "I don't give a fuck" perspective and marched to the beat of their own drum. Someone who incorporated the ideals of doing what they want, when they want (within legal and appropriate reason, of course).

They'd have friends of all ethnic and gender backgrounds, as the bonds were mostly about being like-minded. Now, as this individual developed, they could certainly become the subject of a shit ton of ridicule and could often be looked at as "other." It may be difficult to fit in anywhere, because the nature of being viewed outside of a box would consistently be at the back of the mind. In hindsight, this was the group I was naturally aligning myself with, although it has been a work in progress. It's not likely that some who possess a real independent spirit can completely embrace themselves during their middle school years. These times are hard enough for those who seem to be comfortable with themselves. But this was the reality. In a sense, it was akin to the "tragic mulatto" syndrome but minus the mulatto factor. Not Black enough for the Black kids and not White enough for the White kids. All while being very Black at the same time. Just weird and in between. And yet, having to learn to accept who you are as an African American with a liberated essence. None of this analysis is solely intended to place Black people into one of the three categorical boxes. People can be an assortment of so many dynamics. It's merely a loose critique of how I saw things as a young teenager. Never telling anyone what I was thinking but simply keeping the observations bolted shut within my vault.

It became commonplace for my Black peers to refer to me as a "sellout" but for no real reason whatsoever other than not fitting into their box. It was equally as typical for my White peers to refer to me as the "Black kid who talked White." And when this description was used, their intent was for it to be taken as a compliment. It was supposed to make you feel special to have the term "White" attached to you. This was, undoubtedly, White supremacy in a horrible disguise. That terminology was in constant usage. It took a lot of restraint not to act out or go buck wild, but the feeling of living in silence kept me restrained. The displeasure of not having anyone to vent to resulted in a lot of frustration, and my parents were emotionally hands-off. To me, family was a nonfactor in terms of having individuals to confide in. I just got used to it.

The feeling of always being in limbo made these entities super uncomfortable to talk about with friends. This tended to sit within my psychosis until the appropriate bond occurred, if the connection ever actually did ensue. Being this way had its ups and downs, for sure. At times I felt like a fraud, which is a feeling that would only get worse as I got older. I had so much inside but wasn't attempting to express any of it. Conversely, there was some solace in knowing that many of these traumatic experiences were leading to the development of some very unique personality traits.

On occasion, the thought that I was becoming more of an individual felt like a low-key superpower. There is a Kid Cudi song called "Immortal" where the first line of the song is "I am the smartest man alive!" Another section of the record has lyrics that say, "I'm living my life as if I've got powers." This is the kind of confidence that was beginning to bubble beneath the surface for me. I wasn't exactly *living* it but starting to feel it. For better or for worse, I felt like I was becoming a bit of an elitist, which is ironic seeing as how I was immersed in circumstances that could have easily led to having an inferiority complex. The television media I was exposed to (as I mentioned earlier) had its effects, and pushed me toward exploring my sense of humor and being more of a "snarky asshole." Feeling displaced drew me toward shows that featured others I considered atypical: *In Living Color, Seinfeld, Martin, The Wonder Years*, etc. A cross section of jerks on camera, so to speak. Times were certainly strange. Was I alone? Was I the only one being seen? Was I being seen at all?

23

It was right around this time during my latter middle school years that I had my first very minor experience with dating. It certainly wasn't dating in a traditional sense, because we couldn't drive anywhere or spend a significant amount of time together, but it was more like an "in school" type thing. There was a half-White, half-Japanese girl named Kimi I had a crush on for quite some time. Probably dating back to elementary school. To my surprise, race was never mentioned by the other students in this particular circumstance. Maybe because the half-Japanese aspect implied some sense of color, and therefore led the other students astray. I recall being enthralled with the way her thighs looked. Super muscular, as she was a runner and a swimmer. She was like a little girl version of the great Brazilian soccer star Pelé. Very athletic body type. We were acquaintances, mainly because of our connection through mutual friends. Kimi and I didn't engage in much one-on-one conversation, but we knew of one another. At the very least, we were on each other's radar.

One particular day, I got the balls to ask her out, which really didn't entail much at all. But I suppose at that age, everything means more than it should. It really does take some gumption to walk up to a young girl and make such a request. My heart rate was going into overdrive. My pits were getting sweaty, which is always a bad look to girls. My speech was slightly delayed, as I was clearly putting off the question at hand. But I got it done and stood in an awkwardly nervous state for the next five seconds. A period of time that might as well have been hours in my middle school brain. To my surprise, she said yes. I don't know if I expected her to say no, but for whatever reason, I was taken aback by her answer. I was happy, shocked, and confused.

What was I supposed to do now? Did I have to step up to the plate and start buying flowers and walking her to and from class? Did I need to show my affection by waiting at her locker on a regular basis and writing her love letters? I was completely clueless. Without a doubt, my state of confusion caused my anxiety to peak and I went into flight mode. Rather than being encouraged by her willingness to date me, I cowered. In all honesty, the two of us spoke more frequently prior to dating than afterward.

The whole situation was weird, and maybe a week later Kimi broke up with me. She didn't do it directly but had a friend come up to me one day after school and break the news. It was certainly strange hearing this news from her friend, but maybe it would have been even odder had I gotten it from Kimi herself, since we didn't really even speak much. Honestly, I wasn't even too bothered, but I did wonder how others would perceive me. After you get dumped, I think it's common to be concerned with how you could be viewed, especially at such a young age within a school setting.

Regardless, I couldn't do anything about it. Life goes on, but I was a tad salty about how it had all gone down, even though I'm certain my fleeting social nature had something to do with it. A few days later, I was hanging out with a neighborhood friend of mine named Xavier. He was part of a military family, just as I was. We called him "X" for short. He was a cool kid I could really relate to, but he was only in the area for a short amount of time. I would have loved for our friendship to have developed, but it wasn't in the cards, logistically speaking. Anyhow, he and I were goofing around that afternoon and decided to give Kimi a call. The reason for the phone call eludes me now, but I'm sure we were just being immature middle schoolers. Actually, I'm fairly certain it was his idea, as I definitely wouldn't have wanted to call her house after what had occurred.

She picked up the phone and engaged in a short conversation with Xavier. He asked her if she'd like to talk to me, and for whatever reason, she said she did (I bet she was fairly reluctant but agreed anyway). I was super nervous, per usual, and had no idea what to say. I don't know what was going through my mind, but I felt the need to throw a slight jab at her because of the way she broke up with me. I didn't have any intent of being malicious, but I did want her to know I was a tad displeased. In a mildly reckless fashion, once Xavier handed me the phone, I stuttered a bit, said hello, then continued to tell her she smelled like fish. . . . Her silence after my erroneous comment said it all. If my brain could have talked to me in that moment, it would have said, "Holy fuck!! What did you just say?!?" I knew I was out of line and hung up the phone in shame.

At the time, I had no clue that saying a woman smelled like fish was truly a nasty insult. My statement would have implied that we had been intimate on some level, which was the furthest thing from the truth. We had barely even spoken or even seen each other in school. I suppose one could have interpreted my comment to have been on the more prejudiced side, the implication being that she smelled like a Japanese fish market (which would have been a total stretch for me to connect the two). But to be honest, my fish comment was simply intended to reference the fact she was an avid swimmer. And of course, fish and swimmers both make their living in the water. My little joke had gone horribly wrong and been taken out of context. I should have known better, I guess, but my youthful ignorance was put on blast. All of our mutual friends at school gave me shit about it for weeks.

I was the butt of many facetious comments, all of which I deserved. Some people started calling me "fish boy." Others would walk past me in the halls and ask me what I was having for dinner, with the implicit intent being that "fish" would be the answer. I knew it would all blow over soon, but my awkward middle school demeanor had really been exemplified. Now, I view the moment as a hilarious misstep, but at the time it made me very uneasy. As much as my burgeoning individuality was aiding my overall confidence, I clearly had some work to do in terms of socialization. All harm and *all* foul. I had completely, and unknowingly, fucked up.

24

These awkward developments were, without a doubt, unique within my personal experiences during adolescence. But everyone deals with uncomfortable shit during their evolving years. As you can see, one of the most difficult aspects of it all has to be when one begins to harbor some romantic attraction to their peers. When feelings of sexuality come into play. When kids start talking about intimacy, dating, crushes, etc. Although this wasn't the case with Kimi, race was often a notable topic to others. I was slowly beginning to become accustomed to this, although I didn't want to acknowledge it as a reality.

The Black women I had been so positively influenced by in my family were amazing. They were strong, independent, intelligent, and beautiful. But they were family, and at times, even they would make comments about couples and their race when it didn't seem to matter. These comments were mostly said in jest, but it was hurtful to me that people who I had put so much trust in were making erroneous comments that seemed rooted in prejudice. At this point, I hadn't fully developed that part of my sense of humor, so I wasn't prepared to deal with such jokes at face value. Of course I had been exposed to jovial references to race on TV, but I chalked them up to them being funny for a purpose, rather than holding such emotions near to their hearts.

I specifically recall shopping at a mall in Northern Virginia, and my mother and aunt saying "IRC" whenever an interracial couple (which is what IRC stands for) would walk by. One time, a couple walked past consisting of a fairly athletic Black male and an obese White woman. My mother and aunt proceeded to make witty remarks about how this man clearly just wanted to be with ANY White woman, which I supposed was obvious to them because of her weight. They undoubtedly didn't know either of the individuals, but they believed their theory was indisputable. It almost seemed like they were poking fun at these couples because they harbored some animosity. Maybe they actually did. It's never been something we've spoken about. I am well aware that people, myself included, will make offensive jokes with others in private. But in these moments, the jokes were coming out around impressionable ears, which I didn't find to be very responsible. They might not have considered any children were listening. In addition, both of them had staunch views that were rooted in Christianity. Their religious views appeared to be central to how they lived their daily lives, so it seemed completely antithetical to be judging the choices of others with race as the primary component. Ultimately, nobody is perfect, and we all make mistakes. I was just unsure if their rhetoric could be classified as a mistake.

At this point, there weren't too many Black girls in my grade. And for whatever reason, this started to make White girls seem exotic to me. Not exotic in the way the word is denoted. Not foreign or distant but certainly "different." Enough difference to result in a heightened level of intrigue, I guess. Sometimes people become drawn to the "unfamiliar" while others are enticed by what they know.

The media's portrayal of beauty has never included everyone, so it's possible I was a victim of this in terms of my perceptions. Its Eurocentric preferences can aid in shaping perspective, although I personally never felt the need to appeal to this with regards to my own aesthetic. This sentiment shouldn't have mattered at all in a perfect world, because we are all human at the core. But at the time, it did.

This feeling didn't stick with me as I got older, as the "exotic" nature of White girls subsided. One's taste during puberty isn't remotely close to being in its final form. It's more like being in the second season of a television series that consists of eight or nine. Currently, if I refer to someone as "exotic," then I mean it in the manner in which it is defined. With time, I grew to appreciate the beauty of women from all ethnic backgrounds. But back then, I'd voice my feelings (which were mostly platonic) for a White girl and would be met with raised eyebrows. Personally, I didn't care if the girl was White, Black, red, or blue, but everyone else did. In Stafford, it wasn't quite as taboo as it was in Louisiana, but people would let you know how they felt about it. There were a few occasions when I'd go to a platonic White girlfriend's home just to play or study, and the parents would blatantly inquire as to whether or not there was any ulterior motive on my behalf. It seems foolish, but it really happened that way.

In one particular case, I went to a girl's home to hang out, and the rumor mill had already begun to circulate about how her parents felt about Black boys. I hadn't even arrived yet. Her father had apparently seen their daughter at a middle school football game sitting next to a Black student and said to his wife, "This is the last time she will be seen next to a nigger." I guess some kids overheard him and started talking about it. So, there I was, hanging out at her house. In hindsight, she had some pretty big balls. Her father came around, seemingly to spy on our actions. He was actually a pretty nice guy to my face, but he had one of those "old Southern White man" type voices that sounded like he was gearing up for his next Klan rally. I was on edge the entire time. Things ended up being fine, but it was deeply disturbing to know that these kinds of feelings were floating around so casually.

In another instance, I remember being at home with my family right before dinner. I think my father had brought home pizza or maybe McDonald's. Fast food meals were fairly common for us, as both parents worked and went to the gym regularly. I had just finished my homework and was watching MTV. Some sort of evening "wrap up" of the most popular videos of the day. My father dropped the food off and expected everyone to gather around the dinner table and eat as a family. My siblings and I all grabbed our food and went back to doing whatever it was we were previously engaged in. I felt like my father was a bit offended by the fact none of us seemed to want to eat together. I don't know this for sure, but it was just a vibe. At the time, I was more concerned with the music than anything else. There was a Red Hot Chili Peppers video called "Give It Away." It was a hit. A funky record with bluesy and rock undertones. The song was very California-esque and modern, which was a sound my father was not accustomed to. When he noticed I was really into it, I could see the displeasure on his face. He shook his head and said, "I guess White girls are what is coming next." This was surprising to me, as I'd previously never heard him mention race in that manner. It was definitely an interesting caveat though, because a few years prior all he could talk about was how attractive the famous skater, Nancy Kerrigan, was. During the whole 1994 Winter Olympics scandal, Terry was quite vocal about his affinity for her. He never said anything too revealing, but the consistency with respect to his "name dropping" of her was telling. I never mentioned that little conundrum to him, but I felt it inside.

I could see it wasn't only White people who voiced their displeasure at even the slight possibility of interracial relations. Nor was it confined to Black women and White men. It was coming from all over and was a pervasive factor.

In a slightly unrelated event during my fathers' minor "White girl" rant, was that it was the first time he had ever intentionally mentioned anything regarding politics. Toward the end of his "soliloquy," he randomly told me, "A Black person should never vote for a conservative political candidate because they have never acted in good faith toward marginalized communities." It was very much out of the blue but worth mentioning. In a moment, he had rattled off both a conservative talking point and then a more stringent progressive one. Both of which contained new information coming from him. It was definitely something worth my analysis, albeit quite confusing.

Politics are never "black and white" in a general sense, but I was beginning to become a bit confused on the issue. My father's comments rang true with me, even though I didn't think they were totally accurate. It's never a good idea to pigeonhole anyone into a category, but in that short time span, I looked at his words as being kind of gospel. I've never really been one to put my complete trust into anything, politics included.

Slowly but surely, I began to realize political lines weren't *always* drawn with race being at the forefront. In prior generations, race would have been a much larger factor, but not quite as much during the '90s. I am by no means minimizing the role that racial factors have played into legislation. Most situations weren't akin to David Duke running for governor of Louisiana. That would be an outlier, albeit one I was acutely exposed to. I guess we've had Presidents who openly supported organizations that carried out acts of domestic terror. I could have been more confused than I thought. Politics can be ethnically driven, but they don't have to be. I guess the fact most politicians are old White men doesn't help in terms of assuming an anti-racist agenda. My thought process at that time would have definitely been flawed. Maybe in my case, I was engaging in wishful thinking.

Dad always voted democrat but oddly voiced his support for Colin Powell (a four-star general and an African American man who was known to be more of a right winger), in the event he'd ever run for office. Terry said he highly respected Mr. Powell's military background and fiscal perspectives. So, in that sense, I guess he would vote for a conservative candidate if said candidate was a highly decorated Black military veteran? I didn't know for certain, but I kind of understood. Maybe his perspectives were a bit warped. Maybe they were derivative of growing up during the civil rights movement era and placed an ingrained distrust for corporate Whites into his head. I mean, that would make a bit of sense, I think. In hindsight, I wish I had asked him about his thoughts on Clarence Thomas or even O. J. Simpson for that matter. Obviously, OJ wasn't a politician, but you can tell a lot about a person after hearing their thoughts on him as a human being or even general thoughts on his murder trial. The types of conversations we wish we had are often very telling, especially when one is developing as an adolescent.

25

Toxic rhetoric was still constantly coming from within my immediate peer group, which wasn't surprising. Maybe in reality it can all be chalked up to teens being teens. But that aspect didn't make it more digestible. One day, my classmates and I were engaging in what seemed to be a regular conversation on the school bus. It was a normal afternoon, but a friend decided to ask a specifically probing question. It may sound trivial, but she asked if I thought she had a better ass than another classmate. It's important to note the individual asking the question was Black, and the person on the receiving end was White. The asker's name was Anita, while the recipient's name was Meghan. Both were attractive girls. I was friends with them, but didn't harbor any romantic feelings toward either. The question seemed random, but it really wasn't, as Anita would talk about sex quite often. And here I was again being placed in the middle on an issue that shouldn't have dealt with ethnicity but ultimately ended up doing so. Racial disputes were becoming all too common.

One would assume that the answer to the question would be fairly objective, but my objectivity and candor wasn't received that way at all. I answered the question as I saw fit, and the winner was Meghan. It didn't really matter in the grand scheme of things, but in this isolated instance it was a big deal. Anita proclaimed my answer to be pandering to White people. If someone is an ass guy, then they'd all have proclaimed Meghan to be the winner. I say that facetiously, as I am aware that everyone has their individual tastes, but honestly, it was quite obvious. When she wore her tight leather pants to school, I couldn't take my eyes off of her posterior frame. But this wasn't the answer Anita wanted to hear. She was jokingly livid at my response and voiced her displeasure by saying, "You must prefer White flesh!" In my opinion, it was an odd reaction from her because I was supposed to be rating the body part and not the skin tone. That's my analytical side kicking in, as it usually does. With my answer, I was fucked. As argumentatively playful as I am, I had no comeback for her response. I felt like Sonic the Hedgehog when he's running with a full head of steam and has ninety-nine rings but then encounters one little spike and everything goes to shit. I had never experienced this sort of interpersonal defeat before. She played the race card against me out of pure discontent for my answer. I always had an irreverent comeback, but in this instance I was left dumbfounded. I had to take the "L."

26

Early teenage years are often filled with so much we can't understand or process while we are going through them. Depending on one's support system, the highs and lows can be both joyous and scathing, while the in-between moments sit like a placeholder. For many families, religion acts as a bonding unit. Something to tie the family together while simultaneously allowing for an escape from the realities of everyday life. It can also serve as a moral beacon. To teach people how to think, act, worship, and to make sense of the world we live in. At its most basic level, it helps those who follow make sense of the nonsensical. But it doesn't *have* to do any of those things.

We have freedom of religion in this nation, so we can consciously choose not to give any credence to religious principles. It's really up to us as individuals to make these decisions for ourselves and do what works best for us. The notion of freedom of religion inherently implies respect for those who may worship differently, or those who do not worship at all. This respect should be shown on a civic, personal, and governmental level. The Constitution clearly states, "Congress shall make no law respecting an establishment of religion or prohibiting the free exercise thereof . . . " We should have just as much respect for a

Baptist preacher as we have for a member of the Church of Satan. As long as individuals aren't hurting others or attempting to force their views, we should offer deference to everyone's religious perspective or its subsequent nonexistence. Faith is such a personal factor to an individual's life, so to me, it doesn't even make sense to concern oneself with what someone else is thinking. I understand why a parent would want their children to be on the same page as them, but it's the element of force that never sat well with me.

Growing up in a Baptist household, my siblings and I were taken to church as early as I can remember. No questions were ever asked regarding whether or not we would be going. It was expected, and we were coached to follow suit. The services were occasionally entertaining and informative. The congregations were often full of Black prosperity and love. I can honestly say attending church was enjoyable at times.

At one point, my brother and I were encouraged to learn all the books of the Bible and recite them in a catchy singsong manner. Kind of like the ABCs. It was all part of a performance for the church. It was cute and slightly gratifying but mainly because it was challenging. I always wondered why it was so important to know the names of the books without knowledge of the content of said books. Do the names really mean anything without a grasp of why the books hold merit? He and I went through with it anyway and delivered a pretty decent showing. Once all the applause subsided, I went back to dissecting the general actions of the churchgoers. There was always a lingering hint of judgment. If you dressed in a manner that didn't fit the status quo or embodied any aspect of counterculture, you could be silently vilified.

Our grandmother and grandfather on our mother's side were two of the staunchest old-school Christians I've ever been around. I know it was stated earlier, but this lifestyle really reverberated in the way my mother lived (and really how she wanted her children to live as well). The appearance of my brother and I knowing the books of the Bible gave her a sense of pride. As proud as she was of us, my grandmother was even more elated at what we had done. We mailed her a cassette tape of us singing the tune so she'd have a hard copy. I can't really say my dad really cared about our "accomplishment." My father always said he was a Christian, but the optics were quite different with him. I think he believed in God but never talked about any specifics. My personal opinion is he just said the right things because the other members of our family would adversely judge him if he didn't.

27

During grade school, I would make comments questioning certain aspects of the Christian faith. As I approached the later stages of middle school, my desire for answers became far more important to me and concerning to others. I'd ask questions during Sunday School. I'd ask my grandmother questions. I'd ask my mother questions. My goal was always to get into the nitty gritty of some of the most well-known biblical tales, but if something didn't sit right with me, then I couldn't wholeheartedly buy into it. It seemed like nobody had the responses that would quench my thirst. The notion of an omnipotent and omnipresent God didn't make any literal sense to me unless it could be proven without question.

If the stories were all true, then shouldn't we be able to apply them to current times? For example, in the tale of "Daniel in the Lion's Den," God saves Daniel because of his unwavering faith (among other things). So, wouldn't this imply the same could occur today, assuming someone's faith in their creator was so strong? If my grandmother's faith was that intense, she should be content with being placed in a den full of lions, knowing that her higher power will save her, right? Maybe they were just stories, and maybe I'm missing something, but nobody would ever come

out and simply say that. I fully admit I could be making an ignorant assumption by connecting events that allegedly occurred
during biblical times to potential modern situations. However,
the concept of having faith in the existence of God just wasn't
ever going to be in the cards for me, and once I came to terms
with that I felt I could make an accurate decision on how I'd
worship.

The result: I wouldn't worship at all. I couldn't summarily
dismiss the existence of God, as I didn't feel I had the ability to
obtain such knowledge, nor do I think I ever will. But it was also
impossible to prove, without a doubt, that God truly existed. It's
this outlook that caused me to take on the viewpoint of an
"agnostic individual who leans atheist." This triggered some
turmoil between my mother and myself because it was at this
point I began to push back at the idea of attending church
services. It didn't make any sense to go if my mentality didn't
align with their messages and/or practices. I didn't even believe
in the actuality of the Supreme Being they deemed to be the
creator of the universe. This belief system still resonates with me
now. I will always support those who believe or show their devo-
tion differently and expect the same treatment from others.

28

In the midst of so many off-putting relational dealings was the obvious fact that during these years, one begins to struggle with sexuality. I'm not necessarily referring to struggling with whether one is gay, straight, bisexual, etc. Although those could be, and often are, elements of one's plight. I'm more speaking on the nature of wondering about and/or acting on sexual desires and all that doing so could entail. Questions about how it will all go down. When will it happen? With whom will it happen? Will the situation be pleasurable? What is a make-out session like? What is oral sex like? What does a woman smell like (which, by the way, is a question that will never deliver a clear-cut answer)?

From a young male's perspective, I know my friends and I would talk about what it would be like to finger a girl, although it might sound juvenile to admit. It's actually pretty funny to me that I even wrote about that specific act. But it's all part of sexual development. For myself, an interesting caveat was thrown into the mix, as I was exposed to hardcore pornography starting in the fifth grade. The primary impetus to this was because my father had bought a device called a descrambler. The basic principle behind it was that it unscrambled all of the extra movie channels that weren't being paid for as part of your cable package. In those days, non-paid channels still showed up on your television, but they were visually scrambled up. The descrambler gave you access to them all, which included all of the pornographic networks. For us, the main one we had access to was the Playboy channel. I still remember seeing it for the first time like it was yesterday.

A time for me that will live in infamy. Channel 25. My life would never be the same. Prior to this, I had seen movies I really wasn't supposed to watch. I'd seen love scenes that definitely had sexual implications, the most intense of which was in a Jean-Claude Van Damme movie called *Double Impact*. I remember there being lots of smoke and a sultry-looking red background. Body parts weren't really shown, but the overall connotation was clear. I know it may be cliché to say again, but there are levels to this, and I had definitely hit a new level. To be honest, I was completely mesmerized. As a young male that was going through so much sexual curiosity, I was now presented with almost everything I was ever questioning through a visual medium. Ranging from multiple positions to oral sex, anal sex, girl-on-girl sex, etc. There was also a lot of interracial sex, which was directly contradictory to the narrative floating around in my real life. Things I was told shouldn't occur were all of a sudden right in front of me on a continuous basis.

My personal favorite actresses were Nina Hartley, Kobe Tai, and Heather Hunter. The entertainment I was getting from the Playboy channel was far superior to what I was getting from any other network. But obviously I couldn't really watch it at my leisure. I was always sneaking around trying to catch a glimpse whenever my parents were gone. Then I concocted a strategy that would benefit me for years to come. I used to get home from school about twenty minutes before my brother and sister. I'd turn the Playboy channel on as soon as I arrived and start recording whatever they were airing (using the many blank VHS tapes we had laying around our house). I would only record material for roughly fifteen- or twenty-minute increments. There wasn't enough time for much else. In fact, the only reason we had so many blank VHS tapes at our disposal was because my father had advised me to utilize them to tape tennis matches in order to study the moves of some of the greats. I had ulterior motives and would slowly amass hours of pornographic footage that I could watch in my room with far more comfort. Unfortunately for me, not everything I recorded would be classified within the category of hardcore porn as I defined the term. About a quarter of it was material like celebrity centerfolds or softcore B movies. I couldn't stand either of these, as I viewed them as a waste of space on my tapes. But it was worth taking the hit in order to have the material I really desired. Those were some fun times. At one point, I was even able to pinpoint the EXACT moment when one of my recordings transitioned from an intense tennis match to an erotic porn scene and could turn the tape off at the drop of a hat. My skills in that arena were crazy good!

A major conundrum regarding this newfound exposure to adult entertainment as a child was that my parents never, not even once, broached "the birds and the bees" talk. I don't think I ever even heard the word "sex" brought up by them at all. To be completely honest, I often wondered if the two of them ever had fruitful sex, in the sense of being sensual and gratifying to both parties. Was the notion of hot sex a complete non-starter with regards to their relationship? My brain will never become inundated with such candor. I feel like when most kids hit puberty, they sort of brace themselves for the moment when their parents will talk to them about romantic endeavors. It isn't a comfortable feeling in the least. It hangs over your head like a chandelier ready to snap and fall at any moment.

Even though the situation is filled with apprehension, you kind of want it to happen so that you can get it over with. You're also curious to know how your parents feel about sex in general. Will they be more on the carefree, hands-off side? Or will they be conservative and act like nothing but negativity can come from the act? Maybe they will meet somewhere in the middle? Most of my peers' parents were all over the place when it came to the issue of sex. Some were very aware it was going to happen, so they just preached safety and advised the use of precautionary measures. Others were adamant about abstinence. The latter were more likely to be the ones that made their kids' friends leave their home at about 8 or 9 o'clock, fearing that only acts of immorality occurred after those hours. These were generally the parents with strong religious backgrounds. That's not to imply anything disparaging about their particular ideals, but I'd be lying if I said that it didn't include components of sexual suppression.

I had one friend in particular whose parents were like that, and she was obsessed with staying a virgin. This obsession didn't subdue her sexual desires, as she did date around. I knew some of the guys who had dated her, and her personal solution to staying a virgin was to only engage in anal sex. I guess that worked for her. Maybe not? I don't really know, and I'm not sure how that works in terms of maintaining one's virginity. But everyone has their own personal kinks.

I had other friends whose parents were aware their child was having sex, and they preferred that it occurred in their own home under their "watch." The spectrum was fairly wide, but my parents never even mentioned it, so I didn't know where they stood. I can assume my mother would have been a staunch supporter of abstinence, given her religious views, but I can't be 100 percent sure. I'm sure my father wouldn't have cared much either way. The irony was that our home was basically filled with access to pornography 24/7. I guess it's pretty funny in hindsight.

Contrary to popular belief, being exposed to such explicit material didn't turn me into a sexually deviant individual. I didn't become obsessed with sex or infatuated with acquiring it. In all honesty, it actually scared me a bit. After all, these were pros I was watching, and at the time, what they were doing didn't seem attainable for me. There was the intimidation factor. In retrospect, I can honestly say it might have made me more comfortable with casual relationships that were primarily based on physical intimacy, rather than an intense romantic connection. I use the term "might" because I can't be 100 percent sure my level of comfort with said relationships was attributed to the exposure to pornography. It could have also made me more accepting of the sexually deviant lifestyles of others, which I view as a positive. Maybe it's caused me to want to explore sexual situations that would be considered abnormal. I don't really know how to objectively analyze that, as I'm not sure what normal sexual situations consist of. I can make assumptions, but that doesn't make them accurate, although it does cross my mind.

Needless to say, I was very glad I had those stacks of porn-filled VHS tapes in my closet. They really helped as I was continuing to develop. Those times would have been hard for anyone, let alone someone who was struggling within a society that consistently left them feeling out of place. But at the very least, I had visual material that would help pacify me while entering what some would consider the most sexually frustrating time in a young person's life.

29

These years undoubtedly carry with them so much back and forth in terms of poignant moments. Everything within your life seems to be coming from everywhere. From all angles and from every little crevice. Some days it all makes perfect sense, and on others there is nothing but disconnect all around you. So many impactful entities are being thrown in one's direction, while the receiver is ill equipped to internalize what they are being inundated with. Confusion and general perplexity is at the root of so much. You're not mature enough to deal with what's happening in the here and now, nor is your brain fully developed in order to properly contextualize the factors that are influencing your own life.

The concept of death was something I hadn't ever had to deal with up until that point. Not within my own family, loved ones, or with respect to any of the major celebrities that were my proverbial heroes. On the night of September 13, 1996, my father took a friend and I to a football game up in Washington, DC, between his alma mater, Hampton University, and their rival, Howard. His name was Parry. Overall media schtick referred to the game as, "Who's the real HU?" Obviously in reference to the fact that both colleges contain the letters "H" and "U" in their names. It was a great time and contributed to some solid male bonding between all of us. On our way home from the stadium, the radio DJ made an announcement that Tupac Shakur had passed away as a result of gunshot wounds he suffered days prior. This was in the midst of the whole "East Coast vs. West Coast" beef. A complete media projection gone wrong.

I wasn't a huge Tupac fan at the time, but I was aware of his status as a major hip hop superstar. His most recent release was the double album *All Eyez on Me*, which was a mainstay in my cassette player. It was widely assumed that Pac would recover from his injuries, as he'd been shot before and seemed to recover just fine. His resilience was uncanny. But in this instance, he wouldn't be so lucky. The man was only 25 years old. I don't know how the others in the car felt, but I was pretty shocked. This was the first time an artist who I was a general fan of had passed away. Following the announcement, the DJ committed to playing nothing but Tupac's music for the remainder of the night. My dad then persisted to turn the music up and let it ride for the rest of our trip home. None of us even said another word. I wasn't expecting this type of reaction from him. He knew I was a fan of hip hop, but I figured he would just turn on the local smooth R&B station or something.

Although all conversation ceased, the fact that he kept Tupac's music on seemed to me like the act of extending an olive branch to us as young teens. He and I never spoke about it, but that's the vibe I got. It was kind of like an unspoken "bromance," even though none of us shared our thoughts on what had occurred. I think we all have moments like this in our lives. Where something significant occurs that we completely over-look in the moment. Looking back on such occurrences with our eyes wide open can really provide us with a lot of internal clarity. I don't know if it's important to note that Parry was a White kid and a good neighborhood companion of mine. Actually, he was the biggest hip-hop head I knew. As a bit of an aside, he and I used to hang out at his place after school and listen to all the latest rap records. We'd sit and vibe out to the whole No Limit Records catalog, Cash Money stuff, Fat Joe, and Bone Thugs. Those were good times. But throughout the entire night, even given that we were at an HBCU game, nobody ever mentioned race. Once again, a beacon of hope, maybe? This lack of acknowledgement was something I really respected from my father. Even though race is at the forefront of so much that occurs in life (as it should be), it's not *always* a factor, and I think that should be okay to recognize. At the end of the day, we're all just human beings trying to relate and get through life. If only it were that simple.

30

Transitioning into high school definitely offered up some consequential advancements. I attended North Stafford High, and at the time, it would have been considered decently diverse. The changes were slow but impactful. The continued rise of African Americans into the area was constant, so things kept *looking* better, but it didn't seem to be leading to much diversity of thought. Many of these changes were due in part to my growing acceptance of self. Athletics played a large role. My increased involvement in tennis was getting pretty serious, which was a major confidence booster. One of the most endearing aspects of tennis is once one starts to take the sport seriously, you realize you're fighting by yourself on a daily basis. You learn how to lose alone, and you become adept at winning alone. When things get intense, or when you have questions about what moves to make, you have to rely on yourself. Your own intuition takes precedent.

Outside of the great cardiovascular workout playing tennis provided, the independent mental game was what appealed most to me. This was the primary reason I wasn't too high on playing doubles. Too much going on and too much excess room for error. Also, my net game sucked ass, so I was a liability there.

Fighting alone was what I had been doing since I was about six, so it felt like "my normal." When you experience success in a sport that requires *you* to rely on *you*, it helps you discover who you really are. It assists in personality development. It even aids in what you are willing to let others see with regards to yourself. The nature of the game really sharpens you.

If you're upset during a tennis match, it would behoove you not to let your opponent notice. The result could be that it is used against you. Or, in a worst-case scenario, exposing yourself could lead to your own implosion. Some players are perfectly okay with exposing that part of themselves on the court, or maybe they just have such a difficult time controlling their emotions. In very rare cases, having emotional outbursts can fuel outliers to perform at an even higher level. In those scenarios, it's more natural to show that side than it is to contain it. I made the conscious decision to behave in a mentally restrained manner. It wasn't in my nature to act out when it came to general life situations, and that perspective translated into a similar demeanor on the court.

Because of the appealing nature of fighting alone, I began to find peace in keeping a considerable amount of time to myself. Some might call it being detached from others, while I would say I was finding extreme comfort from within. I guess it's the balance between the two that was most needed. The search for that stability would be like locating a four-leaf clover for me. Even with this being the case, I always felt like it would be far better to be too detached from situations than to become overly connected with them.

It felt amazing to learn how these minor nuggets of perspective could be applied to my own life. As athletics and academics became magnified in high school, merit became a bigger deal than I'd ever noticed. Far more integral than how it played out in the schoolyard football fields of Louisiana. I was no longer seen as "Justin Marlowe, the confused oddball." Now I was "Justin Marlowe, the kid who will kick your ass on the tennis court." Or "the kid who's in the top 5 percent of his class." The major psychological issue was that I still felt like an oddball inside. My growing inner confidence would manifest on the tennis court at times but not so much in my day-to-day life. Not having any real like-minded individuals around me was still an impetus to my own mental freedom. Although my overall self-assurance had never been higher, it didn't feel that way most of the time.

A coping mechanism I used was to delve further into my musical influences, which seemed to be broadening by the week. Groups like Ace of Base, Madonna, and Soundgarden were becoming mainstays in my CD player. My taste for hip hop also continued to grow, and I became fairly obsessed with Snoop Dogg, Bone Thugs-N-Harmony, Biggie, Jay-Z, Redman, and Tupac. When I'd ride to tennis tournaments with my father, he'd often keep R&B radio stations on, so I was inundated with the likes of Jodeci, New Edition, and Sade. When it came to acts that would be considered pure pop, Ace of Base was pretty much all that I listened to, other than a bit of Wham!, while living in Germany. I use the term "pure pop" to denote artists that weren't much of a blend of anything other than what would have been considered commercially viable to a predominantly White audience. Michael Jackson, Prince, and George Michael (as a solo artist) all meshed a healthy blend of R&B (and sometimes rock) into their music, so I don't quite pigeonhole them into the pop category. On the other hand, my sister, Shayna, was very much into unabashed pop music. At this time, her mainstays were NSYNC and the Backstreet Boys.

I didn't think her personal choices would impact me at all, but they definitely did. Once, I recall stealing a couple of her cassette tapes, both of which were albums by the aforementioned artists. They were the debut albums by each group, respectively. Honestly, I don't really remember why I did this, when I could have just saved up and bought the albums myself. Maybe I thought buying a couple of albums by boy bands would make me look soft. If that was the case, I should beat myself over the head for such a decision. Irrespective, in doing so, I became exposed to groups that would become cultural mainstays for me for the next five or six years. These two acts completely changed my perspective on popular music. Their records were instantly appealing, because they were sort of mixed like rap records. Their drums hit hard and the highs were accentuated. Their production was handled by Swedish musicians, some of which were the same producers who had worked with Ace of Base. This similarity resonated heavily with me. The vocals were carried by lead singers that could rival the greats. It was pop music, but it borrowed just enough from R&B acts like Boyz II Men to make it feel a bit Black-ish. As much as I wanted to dislike the music, because of the stigma that came with liking boy bands, I couldn't deny the records. They had a vibe I couldn't escape. The strange part was I knew that if I was vocal about being into this brand of pop music, it would once again place me into a cross section of the microcosm of high school society. And that's exactly what it did.

I openly referenced my affinity for the music. My father was cool enough to take our family to an NSYNC concert in Richmond, Virginia. It was their first significant tour of the United States. We didn't realize the magnitude of it at the time, but their opening act was a little-known teenage upstart by the name of Britney Spears. The whole thing was a remarkable experience. I can't even begin to describe how ear-splitting the volume of the fans was. The hysteria was immense. When I told my peers about it, all they could focus on was how "gay" it made me look. This isn't to imply that being gay is bad at all. Unfortunately, during the late 1990s, people used the term "gay" to be synonymous with words like "stupid" or "lame." My personal issue with it was that it was clearly being used as a means to classify me as "other" and to disparage something they didn't understand. The obvious larger impact of using such a term was that it was taking a shot at the slowly emerging LGBTQ+ community. Was it somehow a symbol of lacking masculinity to attend a boy band concert? It's certainly a bit of a paradox, because those types of concerts are primed for meeting girls. I guess it was another example of humans generally wanting to place individuals into a box. If you didn't fit into one, then the perception was that you were worthy of being marginalized. I really didn't care that they were calling me gay, because what I was doing was appealing to me and my artistic senses. But in all honesty, I did care. The paradox existed because I didn't fully possess the tools at the time to not care if I'm being completely honest.

My mother's perspective on art was completely contradictory to that of the other members of my family. I was obviously falling in love with music at this point in my life. My tastes were very wide, with a growing appreciation for a burgeoning pop sound, but I was developing a serious love affair with hip hop. Rap was becoming my genre of choice, as it spoke to me with such veracity. Seeing that the vast majority of its creators were young and Black added a sense of pride to each listening session. They were also edgy, which separated them from most of the individuals in the R&B genre. The way in which their lifestyle was projected was like bait to me. The jewelry, cars, women, and overall gaudiness was so dope. The unattainability added to the allure of the music. This was actually the first time that I recall my brother, Jonathan, and I really connecting. We used to wake up before school and turn on *MTV Jams*. We liked many of the same records, which was comforting from a bonding perspective. From my recollection, the most consistent staple was Bone Thugs-N-Harmony. Their tracks "The Crossroads," "1st of tha Month," "Foe tha Love of $," and "Thuggish Ruggish Bone" used to blare from our television speakers in the a.m. This was my first exposure to the subgenre of hip hop called horrorcore. I felt like my mother couldn't stand these musical choices. The majority of what we were vibing on seemed offensive to her, as her religious upbringing might have made it impossible for her to embrace this type of art. I think the root of her reactions likened themselves to how she was cultured growing up.

Maybe the situation was analogous to parents in the late 1950s who were disgusted with their children listening to Elvis or Chuck Berry types. My problem wasn't that she didn't like the music. People have the right to enjoy whatever they want to enjoy, and not everything is for everybody. The issue I had was that there was no attempt at embracing what her children were clearly influenced by, regardless of her personal feelings. On numerous occasions she would ask us to turn the "noise" off. She wasn't even willing to acknowledge the material as music, only as noise. At the root of her claim, any type of music would have to be classified as "noise" because all sound contains noise. The most Jesus-thumping Christian record would still, without a doubt, be considered noise. I realize she would frown upon their use of profanity, but she wouldn't have even had the opportunity to hear them using such language. Everything she would have been exposed to would have been edited and inherently wouldn't contain any cursing.

It was most likely the overall feel of the music that she was adverse to. Hard, aggressive, irreverent, and very urban. A new type of urban, which she wouldn't have been used to. I feel like in her world "urban" would have meant the "Philadelphia sound" of Gamble and Huff. Records by Billy Paul, The O'Jays, The Jacksons, and Teddy Pendergrass. An urgent street sound that was simultaneously socially conscious and intrinsically wholesome. This new era encompassed victims of the crack era who were telling their respective street tales. Art that imitated life. Either way, I found the non-attempt of her exploring what it was all about to be offensive. Especially since it was something quickly becoming a major influence on the lives of her children.

My father was a bit different. He was primarily an R&B guy, but he did make an effort to modernize his tastes. I can't be sure if it was because he was trying to relate to his kids or if he actually enjoyed hip hop. Whenever all of us were in his car, he would put the urban music stations on. Sometimes he would even ask me to pass my headphones over to him so he could check out what tapes or CDs I was playing. Once, I was reluctant to do so because the song I was listening to was called "Some Bomb Azz Pussy" by Tha Dogg Pound. I handed them to him anyway. He smirked a bit, gave me a perplexed look, and then handed them back to me. The response wasn't a significant gesture, but it meant a lot. Another case of him putting forth some effort in terms of his desire for relatability.

31

Socially, things only appeared to get tougher as my level of openness increased. There was a new television show on MTV that had me fucked up. It was pretty much everything I had embraced from a musical perspective rolled up into a one-hour-long TV program. The show was called *TRL*, which was short for *Total Request Live*. Its host, Carson Daly, seemed cool because even though he had this "regular guy" persona, he was able to successfully relate to a wide array of guests. His on-air presence was perfect for that type of programming. I watched it every day once I got home from tennis practice. And it wasn't just something I kind of wanted to watch. It was more like a necessity. A program I really looked forward to. Somewhat of a daily essential. The major selling point was that it gave the fans a chance to vote for the videos that were played. The ones that garnered the most votes landed higher on their charts. But it was more the eclectic nature of the videos that really fascinated me. Within an hour, I could be exposed to videos by Britney Spears, Wu-Tang Clan, Jewel, Madonna, Eminem, and Marilyn Manson. On one hand, this blend of music was exactly what I needed, as it helped give me the validation I wasn't getting from my peers. On the other, it served as a divisive element that further placed me into the package of being unlike almost anyone else.

On the opposite side of watching *Total Request Live* on a daily basis was that of the BET show called *Rap City*. As I saw it at the time, this particular video program didn't cater to overt musical genre diversity at all, which was completely okay, because it didn't have to. Initially when I started watching, the host was a guy named Joe Clair. He was hilarious and was clearly a student of hip hop. After his departure, Big Lez and Big Tigger took on the role. Each of them had a certain quality that allowed them to be their true selves on air. Or at least it appeared that way to me. They were each great at their jobs.

Even with the show being completely hip-hop based, it still broke the genre down into multiple levels of rap subgenres. Although each and every subgenre wasn't especially appealing to me, it did expose me to artists I wouldn't have initially been privy to. Individual acts such as Jeru the Damaja, Black Star, and Bahamadia would have never been on my radar had it not been for *Rap City*. I suppose I could have randomly previewed some of their CDs while shopping at the Marine Corps Exchange after being forced to go to church on any given Sunday. But that would have been unlikely. I really valued the fact it was so hyper focused on rap. Watching it on a regular basis became absolutely enthralling. That show embodied the antithesis of *Total Request Live* but still resonated with me in a manner that made me feel like art could be freeing. So much amazing music in such a short amount of time. The show had a segment where the artists would go into a booth and freestyle. I think it was actually called "the booth." The process gave the viewer access into the extemporaneous element of hip hop. It started to become a major part of who I was, as I was a mixture of so much. I loved it but cringed at it all at the same time. It felt like being in developmental artistic purgatory.

Having varied tastes in the late '90s wasn't really a cool thing to possess. Here we go again with not being Black enough for the Black kids or White enough for the White kids. Sitting in my own little bubble. Not only that, but I wasn't actively trying to capitulate to either group. For me, it was mainly about finding a place where I could exist as my own person without judgment. I didn't care about being called gay, but I wasn't actually gay. I didn't care about being condemned for any of my choices, except for the fact there was no reason for any of it. Even finding friends I really identified with seemed unlikely, as it was apparent that most people stuck to the places the world carved out for them.

None of what I'm saying is meant to convey the notion that I didn't have any friends during this period. I did have some, and they were both ethnically and culturally diverse. But there was usually too much disconnect for anything to resonate heavily. Never a situation that garnered a legitimate and long-lasting best friend, by conventional standards. It wasn't tumultuous, but it was never really spot on. I was never given what I needed, and in turn couldn't give what others needed. I'm not making excuses, but just speaking candidly. The feeling of being stuck never left.

High school was better than middle school, which was better than elementary school, but not wholly conducive to my development. Even with this being the case, one must continue to evolve. You have no choice. Remaining stagnant will warrant at least *some* minute interpersonal growth. I'm proud that I was still able to succeed. I was able to fight my way into the Virginia State High School tennis tournament. I kept a top-thirty ranking in the Mid-Atlantic tennis division of the United States. I became a Governor's School academic standout. I readily maintained a 3.8+ grade point average. All of this while moving closer to finding a sense of self but never fully obtaining it. The cards life hands us can be quite intriguing at times, can't they?

32

That's me in a nutshell, up until roughly the eleventh grade. So much of who I became was based on how I was cultured. Personally, I feel like most people don't properly analyze the term "culture." Many aspects of how we are raised play into how we are cultured. The term is usually looked at in reference to race, religion, creed, sexual orientation, etc. But it really goes much deeper than that. Most of my general dealings as a child came by way of my father, and I've really come to terms with the fact that I'm really my daddy's son." I think I would have benefited from more balance in terms of parental influence. My mother rarely shared anything substantial regarding her personal life, which certainly limited the depth of connection that could have been obtained. She did, however, help out a lot when it came to my tennis training. Taking me to and from practice sessions and occasionally attending some of my matches. Those were surely endearing efforts on her part. But I would have loved more of an adherence to open-ended discussion. Not having the feeling of judgment when bringing up an uncomfortable topic. There should have at least been more preparatory conversations in order to brief one on potential cataclysmic life events. These would have been ideal, but people can only deliver what's in their proverbial tool kit. If you don't have the hammer, then you can't pass the hammer on to someone else.

I am by no means suggesting that I would have preferred them to have embraced the "snowplow parenting" ideology. They would have had to remove all significant obstacles from my path in order to mitigate any adversity. Employing said method would have been even more of a detriment to my youthful development. That perspective would have been completely "hands on" and generally antithetical to what was available in their cultural tool kit.

My parents did a solid job exposing me to some of the more standard elements of Black culture, and this was a blessing. The movies, TV shows, notable celebrities, etc. But there were key components to African American counterculture that I think were purposely kept away from me. This was, of course, until I could seek them out on my own. My current assumption is that they were both just doing what they knew to be acceptable, without too much intent. A good parent should keep their children away from material they deem harmful. It's just a matter of perspective. I also tend to forget the fact that the two of them were both working full-time jobs, dealing with three kids, and the pressures of trying to mend a marriage that *may* have been approaching the early stages of disorder. Although it was frustrating at times, I can't really blame them for it or hold any animus toward their actions. I can certainly analyze it from my perspective, though. But like I was saying, culture runs much deeper than the ethnic/racial/sexual orientation conjectures that are normally associated with the term. If my parents were cultured in a certain manner, or manners, then that would obviously affect how they attempted to culture their children.

There is military culture. Urban Culture. Suburban culture. Wealthy culture. The cyclical culture of poverty. The culture of women. Hip hop culture. The culture of racism and/or general thoughts of supremacy. I could certainly go on and on, as the term is excessively broad. None of these are ever 100 percent concrete and are subjected to the context of those who are living it and/or speaking about it.

Micro cultural concepts really encompass so much that we typically don't think about, nor do we (in a general sense) properly scrutinize them. Looking back on aspects of life, it's obvious how our families can shape so much of who we are. I never thought much about it as a child, but as an adult I find myself thinking about it quite often. For me, it harkens itself back to the nature vs. nurture discussion. Nurture always seems to win out. I was who I was because of so many elements that had nurtured me. In the same sense, I am who I am today because of what I'd been nurtured by since my teenage years, in addition to what I experienced as a child. Nature seemed to be far less important. That's just my personal opinion. Other than my siblings, I hadn't encountered anyone I felt was my equal, in terms of general relatability and shared experiences. You can take that for whatever it's worth.

There was never anyone of significant merit who could identify with my struggles and vice versa. Even if my struggles might seem minor to some, they were unique to me. And to be honest, maybe I did have friends whom I could have confided in, but I didn't have the tools to properly express myself. We never discussed our inner thoughts at all, and if we did, it would have been extremely rare. It was almost as if we talked about everything except what was inside.

Metaphorically, my siblings and I were like the early artists who were signed to the infamously Black-owned Motown Records, which isn't to impugn their influence or success in the least. Those acts had hits on hits, but the sound was so happy-go-lucky. Bubbly, singsongy, melodic, and carefree. Yet the circumstances surrounding the reality of many of the artists was steeped in the struggle of the Black experience, among many other dire situations. So much was done for us as kids that it was almost as if something was bound to get consistently neglected. And the piece that was ignored was the mental side.

As great as it had been to live in a fairly diverse environment, it left me feeling a bit stagnant. I think the timing was bad for me. Maybe my mentality was too progressive for the era I was growing up in. My expectations might have been too high. The silver lining was that things were getting better. Sometimes we encounter scenarios that blindside us and end up completely changing the course of our lives. It's kind of like the beginning of *The Facts of Life* theme song. "You take the good, you take the bad, you take them both, and there you have the facts of life." Everything we come into contact with shapes us into our current form. Life can be bizarre, to say the least. Toward the end of the theme song, the singer says with so much intent, "The facts of life are all about you." With a major emphasis on *"you."* There is an emphatic magnifying glass on that one term. The individuality that comes from our experiences is so very telling. Life is so evolutionary and can be extraordinary. One's form today isn't what it will be tomorrow. All of this randomness can inevitably become rewarding . . . or not. It just depends.

As I prepare to take you further along into this journey, it's important to reference the fact that I'll be going back and forth with little tidbits of information to help you better understand my vantage point when it comes to Nicos's tale. At some points I'll make note of shared experiences, which occurred after the fact, but the intent is to place you in a position to better comprehend the story as a whole.

PHASE 2

33

Nicos's origin story starts out diametrically dissimilar to mine. I apologize if the timeline jumps around a tad, but we've moved back to 1983. More specifically, November 24 of that year. Right during the Thanksgiving holiday. His full name is Damenicos John Eaton, but he typically goes by Nicos. His middle name, John, comes after his grandfather. His mother had him as a teenager in Fairfax County, Virginia, at the Fort Belvoir Community Hospital. Nicos's father was not present at his birth, nor was he in a relationship with his mother at the time. In terms of Nicos's name, it's a bit of a funny story, but it was actually misspelled on his birth certificate (obviously by accident).

"Damenicos" doesn't read phonetically at all, yet it makes sense. Many that initially see his name assume he is of Greek origin, but this is far from the truth. As you get to know him, his nickname, Nicos, impeccably fits his personality. In my opinion, it comes off as quirky, unique, and noble. It's amusing how things can work out like that. His mother, Bernadette, had a phenomenal support system around her, even though she wasn't in a stable relationship, in terms of how the average person would view her predicament. As I said, she birthed him without his father being present. In fact, Nicos would never come to really know his dad in a conventional sense. Those are just the cards people are dealt at certain times.

Nicos's grandfather, John Eaton, was an Army guy, just as my father was. He retired from the Armed Forces in 1989 as a master sergeant. In the early stages, he was the primary male figure and influence in Nicos's life and was always held in high esteem within their family. I never met him, but I always felt like I had. John was born in the late 1920s and was a product of the Depression era. His time in the service brought with it some of the same stern rigidity I had been exposed to as a child. Notably, John was a Korean War veteran. A bold soldier who put his life on the line to help alter the shifting global affairs in favor of our allies in Asia. Circumstances during this conflict were cold, bitter, and forsaken. What we go through during our most intense periods shapes who we become later in life. Wartime participants are commonly cut from a very specific cloth. My dad never fought in battle, but because his father did, a bit of this persona indirectly bled into his sphere of influence and then trickled into mine. Terry talked about war from time to time and would reference stories my grandfather told him. These conversations would typically be held during our tennis trips. Usually in the car, going to and from events. I felt like I could relate, albeit not entirely. Maybe it was more wishful thinking on my part.

34

The notion of the illegitimate Black youth carries a very specific and blistering narrative within the United States, much of which is based more on perception than reality. The "fatherless child" bears a stigma regardless of ethnic background, but the narrative feels different when it comes to situations involving Black and brown children. Stereotypes with respect to ethnicity are ever-changing. Socioeconomic and political shifts frequently alter how we view our fellow man.

Following the war in Vietnam, many individuals inhabiting urban centers started to become looked at as less than the sum of their parts. Valiant soldiers were coming home to a society that was a shell of what it had been leading up to their departure. The lack of opportunity, addiction, decimated public school systems, and undiagnosed mental health conditions plagued communities all over the United States, with a magnified hammer being struck upon underserved communities. There was a process of de-industrializing the factories, as well as in the schools. Factory jobs became more difficult to obtain, and kids weren't as likely to be encouraged to graduate with trade certifications. It was all so real and hapless. Also, the COINTELPRO situation within the FBI was wild, in terms of squashing any movement that went against their agenda. Some of which were designed to help those in need. The ghettos that were emaciated prior to the war had become even more grief stricken. The war on drugs slowly turned said societies into little factions that were run like militarily controlled states. Right-wing economic programs completely gutted the poor and left them with little to nothing. Trickle-down economics wasn't benefiting those in dire need. As federal funds lessen, urban education systems start to falter, and the youth don't have much to fall back on. If people aren't engaging in sexual activity any less, and the school systems are crumbling, one can assume irresponsible decisions will be made. This causes domestic life to become adversely affected. Most things that would typically be considered wholesome get tossed into the incinerator. Drugs and gangs infest the cities because genuine pursuit of financial freedom seems futile. The pervasive lack of familial guidance leads children to pursue the gang as their family. And then we are back to typecasting the fatherless child.

The child that is often disregarded as a leader and forgotten. Considered a nonfactor or even a pariah to society. Meant to fade into the chasm of nonexistence. Nevertheless, Nicos's family forged ahead and did what was needed to be done in order to succeed. Occasionally, people dig into the crevices of their own selves and the unique resources at their disposal in order to dispel all that is expected. So often it is the outliers that rise up and dismiss archetypal myths.

35

General matters in the Eaton home were carried out in a fairly traditional manner. Some might call it harsh by today's standards, while others might feel as though it was the perfect way to execute a domestic dynamic. Certainly, a more comprehensive way to raise a family, in the eyes of some, in comparison to how things are done in this era. Excessive amounts of leeway were rarely given. There was a typical manner of doing things that didn't divert much from a strong ethical center and fixed sense of morality. Distinctive standards that would predominantly be deemed acceptable to the majority of those in the military, from an old-school perspective. Rigidity becomes a cyclical staple.

Being in their household gave one a feeling as though everyone was somehow connected to the visitor by proxy of whoever they were visiting. You end up becoming ingratiated as one of them. It was both comforting and off putting for me at the same time. Comforting because it literally made you feel like you were around those whom you could instantly trust and confide in, but off-putting because it was rare (in my case) for another family to make me feel that cared for.

Usually, I was just in and out of the homes of others in terms of visiting with friends. I'd be somewhere for a playdate or a sleepover, and then back to my house. With the Eaton family, I was able to develop a sense of connection with most all of them. The vibe was overwhelmingly warm. To be honest, even though I felt very at home with their family, the off-putting nature was also attributed to the fact they all possessed the trait of unwavering candor, which I wasn't used to at all. It wasn't remotely malicious, but there were times when I felt like they were laughing at me because of my off-kilter reactions to their jovial honesty (I've never done well with disguising my facial responses). In the long run, that ended up being healthy, as it was coming from a warm and healthy place.

Nicos's grandmother, Bennie, was born in Texas during the early 1930s. She was reminiscent of the quintessential maternal type. Firm but fair. A stickler for rules but understanding enough to embrace the personalities of her kin. Possessing a child-rearing style that did not treat each child (or grandchild) equally but instead adapted to their needs on a specific level. The type that wholeheartedly encompassed the "mi casa es su casa" perspective, in terms of how she treated outsiders. It was reassuring to be invited into her house. Once again, it wasn't my home, but it seemed like it could be, especially if I stayed for longer than twenty-four hours. Nothing was too off limits. As a visitor, I was treated like one of the family. I spent about three days there once, and it felt more secure than being in my own residence. At least this is how I remember it. I really didn't want to go back home. Nobody ever came over to the Marlowe household for too long, other than close friends of my parents or other family members. I don't think I or any of my siblings felt comfortable having people over for a significant amount of time. That "open-door" type of reassurance didn't exist for us. Whatever Bennie and John had done to foster their home had long-lasting effects. The environment wasn't quite as firm as what I was used to, but it still had some familiar qualities. A great place to cultivate a family.

Nicos's mother, Bernadette, is one of the most resilient

people I've ever met. She was one child out of ten. Born in Massachusetts, her family relocated to the Del Ray neighborhood of Alexandria, Virginia. Eventually she attended T. C. Williams High School. She sometimes comes off as facetiously merciless, but that's just her seemingly unyielding exterior. Most likely a product of life events and circumstances. At her core, she's a proverbial "care bear." If she were on the 1980s television show by the same name, she'd be Tenderheart Bear, the leader of the crew. Very warmhearted, attentive, and affectionate. So similar to her mother. An extremely radiant smile. Her heightened level of empathy was always something that stood out to me with respect to her dignity, and it clearly bled into her son. She really loves hard from the inside. Developing an attachment to the central aspects of a person, as opposed to whatever was on the surface. Something that took so long to ripen within myself was ingrained in Nicos from the start.

Intrinsic development seemed to mean a lot to her. Almost the complete opposite of the way in which my mother came off to me, yet they both possessed astounding qualities in their own right. During the summer of 1981 she became smitten with a man named Carl Ingram, who would become Nicos's father. When her water broke, her father, John, was cooking in preparation for a barbecue. John took her to the hospital at Fort Belvoir, dropped her off, and went back home to continue cooking the meal. On its face, John's actions appear to be tremendously callous, but maybe given his background, it was more like the status quo for him. It isn't easy to gain accurate insights into the actions of individuals from past generations. The context of so much can be skewed. Since we can't pick his brain about the incident, we are only left to analyze and offer our perspectives. But this is what occurred, and under those circumstances, Nicos was brought into the world, whether we deem the surrounding factors appropriate or not.

Obviously, things didn't work out between his parents, which is such a common tale when it comes to relationships, especially when bearing offspring is involved. Nicos isn't completely aware of what accurately transpired and would prefer to keep it that way. In my personal opinion, that's a respectable decision. I'd probably feel the same way if I were in his shoes.

The deep interpersonal dealings between our parents are often so foreign to the children who end up becoming their products. Sometimes the children are too uncomfortable to inquire, in fear it might upset the apple cart. Maybe any questions will ruffle the feathers that have been so carefully misplaced. In many cases, "displaced" could be an even more suitable term. On the flip side, parents can be unwilling to share such untangled information, as it may make them appear slightly unfit. These types of honest conversations are never easy and often go untouched. But the pain of "non-discussion" can be worse than what would have occurred had a brutal heart-to-heart taken place.

36

Nicos lived in Alexandria as a toddler until the age of five. This was, without a doubt, a part of Virginia that was commonly referred to as NOVA (Northern Virginia). A fairly strong metropolitan hub. Nothing similar to the major cities of the United States like Los Angeles, New York, Miami, Atlanta, or Chicago, but close to it. Right on the outskirts of Washington, DC.

John wanted his family to move about two-and-a-half hours southeast to Hampton. The Tidewater region of the state, which is often referred to as the "757" to denote its area code. One of his aspirations was to align them with Nicos's great-aunt, Dr. Martha Eaton Dawson, who worked at the historic HBCU Hampton University (where my parents also attended). His mother hung back in Alexandria. She found a great opportunity working in the telecommunications field at an event-planning company. Although she was almost three hours away, she helped out with her parents' mortgage in Hampton. Bernadette didn't particularly like the idea, but it was negotiated among all parties that it was the best thing for her at the time. She had just landed a great job and it was thought that her parents would be better suited to raise Nicos for the short term. Sometimes we are put into situations where we just have to do what we have to do in order to get by.

Although John served as Nicos's primary father figure for the time being, it's easy to forget he also had six uncles who were present in his life. A large family can sometimes serve individuals very well in the absence of other essential influences. In addition, some of his neighbors were equipped with strong males in their homes who could assist with fruitful guidance for him.

Relocating is never easy for anyone, but in this case, we're talking about a young child who was uprooted from his mother and moved hours away to be with his grandparents. His feelings were all over the place. Nicos was old enough to know why he was leaving but young enough to still be a tad naïve to the entire process.

I know I've mentioned the level of coziness their home provided, but their neighborhood carried many of the same secure characteristics. In general, it would be classified as a typical middle-class suburb. Nothing too crazy or upscale looking but also nothing that looked remotely impoverished or downtrodden. The area was very green. Lots of shrubbery and well-kept yards. Blue shutters on the houses always caught my eye, as I'd never noticed those before. The blue was a particular hue that contrasted greatly from the overtones of the rest of the exteriors. Obviously not every home had the same design/color scheme, but sometimes certain oddities are impactful from a visual point of view.

The area was mostly populated by White people, which was common in 1980s and '90s suburbia. A natural consequence of White flight from urban centers, which was, in turn, a consequence of the Great Migration from rural America (mostly from the Southern states). Situations like this could often put the marginalized individuals in precarious situations. When it was all said and done, we could chalk them up to our learning experiences as we grow, but that doesn't make any of it easier to deal with as they are being experienced in the moment.

While Bernadette agreed to help with the mortgage from afar, this decision didn't come without stiff consequences. When a young child lives with his grandparents, there is an instant disconnect in age. Sometimes all of the love in the world can't replace relatability, in terms of generational closeness. It doesn't mean the condition won't be fruitful, but it can pose substantial challenges. Although Nicos was being raised by his grandparents, his mother wasn't around to provide what would be considered a typical maternal role for her son. This isn't inherently problematic at all, but according to Nicos, it did cause her a significant amount of guilt and regret.

While he was with trusted family members, her influence wasn't as keen as she might have liked it to be. A mother's love for her offspring often extends to being present during their most notable moments as a child, especially during their school-aged years. In many cases, this period can really set the tone for so much that occurs later in life. Personally, I don't feel like my parents' manner of nurturing has ever fully left me. A large segment of who I am is still the little kid in Stuttgart, Germany. I've definitely evolved, but at times my actions aren't too different from what I would have done at the age of five or six. It's had its positive and negative side effects.

In the case of Bernadette, Nicos feels like her lack of parental involvement during that time led her to feel as if it turned him a bit too callous. Like maybe it caused him to feel like he needed to be far more independent than a young child should have needed to be. I'd argue otherwise, but I'm just conveying his testimony.

37

As Nicos grew into being a juvenile in Hampton, he was carrying out life activities that would typically have been reserved for older children. Washing his own clothes, getting up for school without help from others, and using his own transportation (via bicycle) to get to school. These entities could be a product of the times, as general childlike independence was more of a thing during the early 1990s. But it doesn't negate the fact that it's important to note. Many kids from that generation played outside without any fear of inappropriate adult intrusion. We didn't wear bike helmets or knee pads. We'd skate on our rollerblades down extremely unsafe hills with reckless abandon. Accruing scars or minor injuries were like badges of honor. Skateboarding in places we shouldn't and playing tackle football on a daily basis were all commonplace activities. Playing in creeks without shoes was an ordinary affair, especially during the spring and summer months. Not to imply that any of these are positive, but it's just the way things were.

Nicos's domestic independence seemed a little different compared to the norm and unique to his living situation. In my life, things had been quite the opposite, as I always had people doing typical life stuff for me. I did, however, walk to school while living in Kansas (but I don't know if that should really count since the school was literally 200 yards from our backyard). For Nicos, living with his grandparents caused a much heavier load to be placed on his shoulders, but he feels like he is a better man today because of it.

At the age of five, he started kindergarten at a private school in Hampton called the Hampton University Laboratory School. Because his aunt Martha worked at the university, he already had an established administrative connection. This was mostly an all-Black school located on the Hampton University campus. Since the school was private, all of the attendees were from fairly well-to-do families. Mostly people who would have been considered middle to upper-middle class. But because of its location and connection with the university, it was referred to as a Black school. Clearly they wouldn't have discriminated against individuals of other ethnic backgrounds, but I'm just speaking on the overreaching nature of the establishment, in terms of who would attend. Given that his aunt was a high-ranking figure at the school, Nicos experienced a bit of nepotism but also thrived while attending. His group of friends was fairly large, as his charisma was starting to bolster. He never cut up or acted out too inappropriately, but when he did, his actions were usually swept under the rug. In retrospect, I wish I had been lucky enough to have such a connection while in grade school.

From his family's perspective, it was important for Nicos to be around other students who looked like him, as would most likely be the case for any marginalized young child. Even though generally referring to a group of individuals as being marginalized doesn't inherently imply they will have similar traits from an optics perspective. Despite that, one *can* start to develop a sense of identity while feeling like something about them doesn't belong. This can rarely be done in its entirety, as so many dynamics can place us into scenarios where we feel like outsiders, which doesn't *have* to have anything to do with race. Maybe it's someone's sexual orientation, general interests, religion, academic prowess, or body type. Any of these, and so many more, can aid in why an individual might feel ostracized. But in my opinion, race seems to be one of the first traits people look at when they make initial judgments. This is an assumption, and I think that there are definitely levels to my previous statement, as the time period and area one is associated with can dictate so much. It's likely that someone from 1940s Mississippi would be more prone to use race as an initial indicator than a person existing in modern-day Oregon. I realize that may seem like a loose theory, but I think it contains significant merit. Maybe it's more of a hypothesis. All in all, initial racial judgments are probably less likely to occur in adults, but children are much more simpleminded and increasingly aware of the obvious factors, especially as they pertain to physical qualities.

In Nicos's case, he was living in an all-White neighborhood while attending an all-Black private school. If one is just beginning to grasp any sort of unbiased perspective on race, then being placed in this situation could severely hinder one's progression. The question of "why" could linger. Why did the kids at school look different from the kids in his neighborhood? Why did the kids in his neighborhood listen to different types of music than the kids at school? Why didn't he go to school with the kids who lived in his neighborhood? Or why didn't the kids he went to school with live in his neighborhood? In his predicament, much like mine, race was actually never really brought up in discussion by the adults around us. It was all left out in the open. Nicos describes these times as being both a blessing and enjoyable. He loved the school and the neighborhood he was living in. He wouldn't have traded it for anything in the world.

If nobody is there who actively engages in conversation about these situations, it is left up to the child to process. This course of events can often be far more toxic than they are fruitful, but they don't have to be. Sometimes not addressing certain issues can leave them open to innocent interpretation. While the term "innocent" is the key word, this could lead to a much less biased perspective, which would be great. In Nicos's case, he was doing very well. For myself, racial strife was present as a school-aged child, but for him it was not. Fair enough. Sometimes living within a diverse environment can be far more connective than it is divisive. There are a litany of factors that can lead to a certain outcome.

38

One very complex narrative I personally noticed amongst peers who had familial connections to historically Black colleges was that the founding of said institutions was never fully flushed out with us. It generally seemed that our parents never had conversations centering on the "why" behind the colleges, which would have been such a vital point of discussion. Once you know why these organizations of Black higher learning HAD to be constructed in order to provide the necessary educational tools to newly freed African Americans, then you have a more ample understanding of their importance. Once you become aware of the level of discrimination that 19th-century Blacks (and centuries prior) faced when it came to simply seeking information, or just acquiring basic academic skills, it gives you such a robust appreciation for the initial goals that these schools were attempting to obtain. Much like what I had experienced, Nicos's family, although deeply connected with Hampton University and its significance, hadn't delved into the inner depths of the components that led to the impetus of the college's creation.

Without this knowledge, it can leave one wondering why they had to have Black colleges in the first place. I use the term "Black colleges" because that is what they are typically called.

Technically speaking, they are open to acquiring attendees from all ethnic backgrounds. When knowledge regarding the "why" isn't there, it can lead some to assume maybe these places were founded simply as comfort spots. One could think in its simplest form, it's just a case of Black people preferring to be around other Black people, which isn't to say having said perspective would be inappropriate. In many instances, it's common for individuals from marginalized groups (or any group, really) to prefer to be around others who are like them. But this "comfort zone" isn't the reason behind the totality of their creation.

Initially, I used the phrase "complex narrative" to describe all of this. It was my choice of words because I recognize how difficult the conversation would be to have with a school-aged child. But just because it's a tough chat to have doesn't mean that you don't engage. Just my opinion with respect to how my brain works. Others may differ, and that's completely fine. All in all, it's just food for thought, in hopes it can lead to a society with more open-minded critical thinkers.

39

As time passed and Nicos entered the fourth grade, his mother decided to remove him from the Hampton University Laboratory School and transferred him to the local public school, Samuel P. Langley Elementary School. This was a slightly strenuous decision for Bernadette to make, given that the change would be quite abrupt. However, her yearly financial expenditure wasn't making a whole lot of sense any longer. In this case, the maneuver from one school to the other was more than simple relocation. In terms of macro analysis, it was just going from point A to point B. But the micro analysis had much more depth. In the metaphorical blink of an eye, Nicos was uprooted from one cultural landing spot to one that was on the other end of the ethnic continuum.

Langley Elementary was a predominantly White school. Nicos wasn't completely aloof from being around large numbers of White kids at all. His neighborhood was filled with them, and they were the friends he'd play with on a daily basis during his leisure time at home. But things are different when the displacement moves one back and forth from educational settings. The social implications are intertwined and woven into a web of additional intricate factors. The way children act when they play outside isn't always identical to how they behave within a school venue. So much was being adjusted, and this was the first time Nicos began to really delve into racial analysis, in addition to feeling as if he was a bit different. His overall awareness was peaking in conjunction with the change of venue. He was starting to feel as though things were "off" but didn't quite know how to vocalize these misgivings.

All of a sudden, his teachers, aides, and administrators were White, whereas they were previously all Black. Said changes don't have to innately cause any problems at all, but in the mind of a growing child they can be baffling. While attending Langley, Nicos's peer dynamics began to shift. Nothing major, but to him, they were noticeable. His personality was starting to take shape into what it would become. His sense of humor, love languages, and overall sense of expression were molding. All of which would become especially one of a kind.

It's typical for kids to take pot shots at each other, even when they aren't intended to be malicious. We've all done it and have had it done to us. But while in Nicos's new environment specifically, he interpreted these jabs as being racially guided. In conjunction with all of these new jabs changing trajectory in his academic curriculum. It was becoming far more focused on language arts and grammar. Disciplines he wasn't comfortable or well versed in. He was, and has always been, better suited to the worlds of math and science. Nicos despised reading aloud in class. He'd sometimes confuse verb tenses, screw up words, and stutter when nervous. All of which can be excruciating circumstances to deal with as a child in class. Two additional kickers were that his aunt, Martha, wasn't there at his new school to shield him from the embarrassment, and he didn't have a male figure who was close enough in age to productively engage with. As he got older, there was no longer anyone to play basketball with. The adult male neighbors had "dried up." Nobody to play hockey or video games with. Even typical conversations that likened themselves toward general male bonding seemed few and far between.

For a minority, it can be difficult to strike back in such a situation, as you're acutely aware of your surroundings as a marginalized human. Unfortunately for him, he internalized this in a manner that manifested itself in anger. This is a common response to trauma. At this point in Nicos's life, he didn't have the tools to express what he was feeling. General malcontent built to a boiling point and he wasn't able to sort out what was going on. Fortunately, he could talk to his mother on the phone on the weekends, but she wasn't actually there with him, which was something he needed at the time. Irate outbursts ensued, and on one occasion he even bent an entire PE textbook in half. It wasn't just any textbook either. I'm talking about one of the thick paperback types. That moment was the pinnacle of him outwardly exhibiting his outrage with respect to what was going on within his world. It wasn't one specific moment that caused this outburst but a multitude of factors that contributed. Frustrations at school compounded with unfulfilled parental needs had taken a bit of a toll. Was he acting out in a villainous manner, or was he a product of a burdensome situation and seeking some form of expression?

Nicos and I conversely internalized and expressed our bitterness differently. I kept most of my feelings inside at my core, whereas he projected. These conditions are never easy, but discussing them openly and placing said stories into a forum to be consumed can ultimately lead to increased levels of solace. So many young people, myself included, could have benefited from some sort of therapy just to help get through our everyday lives. Even when circumstances don't appear to be serious on the outside, they can slowly nip at you. If one never gets an explanation about where they sit within a societal hierarchy, it is almost impossible to know why one stands where they stand.

40

Oftentimes when anger begins to project, it can be nice to have places of comfort to acquire a constructive outlet. In Nicos's case, he had a few. There was his CCD (Confraternity of Christian Doctrine) instruction, his growing appreciation for popular music, interest in film, and his fascination with comic books. CCD is kind of like a Catholic synonym for what a Baptist would call Sunday school. Because of his grandparents' faith in Catholicism, he basically inherited these perspectives and practices.

Unlike myself, who developed a very anti perspective with respect to religious indoctrination, Nicos found some peace within its instruction and associated activities. He became an altar boy. Most of his close neighborhood friends participated in the same program, so it also became a source of camaraderie. Personally, I only experienced this on minute levels, so religious bonding didn't resonate with me in a powerful manner. To others, it can be very different. For myself, it became like something of a contamination, but for Nicos, it was healthier and helped him form close ties. Good for him on that.

As I rehash certain factors, I find it intriguing how the manner in which we both internalized religion may have affected our mental disposition as adults. I've typically displayed a very obstinate feeling toward so much in life, whereas Nicos had fallen more in line with accepting things in the way the status quo would find acceptable. Our reactions have differed greatly. Our ways of thinking are comparable to me being more punk and him being more hair metal. I love them both, but for very different reasons. Neither outlook is necessarily good or bad (or maybe I should say better or worse) but just an altered way of thinking. I always admire when others can take something that was pushed upon myself and embody it in an entirely different manner. Our respected variances as a human species are not usually appreciated enough.

Secondary to his religious experiences becoming a source of comfort was his appreciation for music. I feel like everyone appreciates the art form, but there are varying degrees of said appreciation. Having known Nicos for the better part of twenty-three years, I can say that the way he treasures his musical influences is quite similar to mine. As a school-aged child, Nicos's grandmother would make him instant oatmeal each morning while watching VH1. This inundated him with the likes of artists like Genesis, Phil Collins, George Michael, Madonna, and Simply Red. Every Tuesday evening, his aunt, Anne, would take him to the local skating rink for "Ladies Night." It was there where he developed an affinity for Taylor Dayne, New Kids on the Block, and Debbie Deb. All things considered, his real favorites were in the genre of R&B. Notable groups like Ready For The World, Boyz II Men, Babyface, and The Deele became central players on his list of personal favorites. And then you have the axiomatic God of music, Michael Joseph Jackson. The King of Pop. Someone who was a pseudo cultural savior during an era when there was so much social uncertainty in the world. Mike almost seemed like a legitimate deity, which is so strange to say about a recording artist. But this was the way it really felt during the late '80s and early '90s. Nicos loved that man's art just as much as I did. He was the type of artist who could do no wrong, even when things seemed to go sideways for him on a personal level. These influences really aided in him making it through some trying situations, just as they had done with myself. So often, exposure to art really helps us in our real lives.

An additional ensuing source of inspiration would be that of hip hop. Much like myself, who became a fan after being exposed to the genres of R&B and pop, rap music became connected to his sense of identity. Not completely, but in more of a pseudo sense. Sometimes seeing Black men expressing themselves in an unfiltered manner can do wonders for the minds of other young African Americans. The art doesn't have to be the same, or even similar, but it's the expression that is the key. In Nicos's case, the adults around him were generally supportive in terms of ingratiating themselves with what he was interested in artistically. There wasn't any condemnation, nor were there pejorative comments. This sort of leeway contributed to a sense of freedom for him. A lot of the time, as young adults, we need to feel free in order to come into our own.

Film and comics provided Nicos with another cushion. Martial arts movies were in heavy rotation and the most note-worthy genre of choice. Actors like Jean-Claude Van Damme, Steven Seagal, Jackie Chan, Arnold Schwarzenegger, Sly Stallone, and Wesley Snipes helped cipher cinematic vitality at times when the outside world appeared increasingly challenging. A few of his favorite movies were *Eraser*, *Demolition Man*, *Bloodsport*, *Kickboxer*, *Pulp Fiction*, and *Rocky III* and *IV*. On the flip side of the action genre was his appreciation for more campy films marketed toward early tweens. Stuff like *Little Giants* or *The Mighty Ducks*. I could completely relate, as my tastes were fairly similar. Most of the aforementioned movies were also staples in my home.

So often, film can be a source of inspiration. A forum for emotional release. Even though we may not be the ones creating them, the fact they are intricately developed artistic pieces helps us formulate our own connection to whatever is being expressed.

The same can be said for comic books. I've never really been a huge fan of them, but I can understand why they arouse so much fascination from others. The visuals alone can be enough to give an onlooker something spectacular to examine. Sometimes the artwork can carry more weight than the stories themselves. Nevertheless, it's the overall escapism that garners so much merit. The chance for the reader to explore moments that seem otherworldly. The opportunity to take hold of characters that are humanoid. They are kind of like us but dissimilar enough to evoke a distinctive type of intrigue. Occasionally taking on alien-like characteristics. Possessing traits that are impossible for mortal human beings to obtain. Superpowers that so many would covet. Every so often, we need elements of fantasy to support our overall maturation process. All of us do it, it's just a matter of the type of imaginative openings we choose to take.

Nicos's favorite comic book hero has always been Black Panther, with other preferred characters being Spider-Man, Batman, and Wolverine. Black Panther's protagonist, T'Challa, is the king of the fictional African nation Wakanda. He has super-human senses, strength, speed, agility, stamina, healing, and reflexes. Pretty much one of the most badass characters in the Marvel Universe. As a nation, Wakanda has superior technological advances compared to its Earthly counterparts. But the most important factor when it came to Black Panther being his favorite was because he was a massively significant African American character. Seeing a Black superhero have so much while still being revered as one of the most respected figures in the comic-book world sat prominently with him. To add a bit of insult to injury (in terms of T'Challa's cool factor), he was married to Storm, the beautiful and courageous weather goddess from the X-Men series. Nicos's comic-book knowledge is pretty vast and encompasses a wide range of heroic, and anti-heroic, characters. Very unlike myself, in terms of general interests and knowledge bases.

When all of these little variations of entertainment and faith are blended, they can really be of service to someone looking for a "daydreaming" aspect in their own life. To some, it might all seem very "pie in the sky," but to others, the teachings and stories can be more palpable than they are erroneous. When one can apply even the most boundless of tales to themselves, relatability starts to kick in. Applicable situations mixed with the extremes that come with fantasy can do wonders for the psychological makeup of some. It can provide hope and motivation where they may have been previously lacking. Maybe on some level, they can even be considered therapeutic. Sometimes we find commiseration in places where we least expect it.

41

While things were progressing for Nicos during his stint at Langley Elementary (he was really finding himself in terms of developmental artistic factors), he described one situation as a bit goofy. A good friend of his was a girl named Bobbie. He had developed a crush on her, and according to him, that spry feeling seemed to be mutual. When describing these pre-teen crushes, it's important to note that they are very much in the vein of shows like *Boy Meets World*. If one looks at the early stages of the relationship between Cory Matthews and Topanga Lawrence, you can see just how childish (and endearing) some of these circumstances were. Very playful and hands-off. A lot of jokes and very adorable displays of light emotional attachment. Acts of intimacy almost never occurred, and the situations were largely based on juvenile physical attraction, conflict, and most importantly, friendship.

Bobbie was a neighbor of the same age who Nicos would engage with regularly. She was a pretty girl, in a typical sense. I don't mean for that to sound pejorative at all. Just not really the exotic or "foreign-looking" type. Dirty blonde hair. Caucasian. Slender build. A smile that was luminescent. The two of them became close. Not quite inseparable but close. He'd hang out at her home from time to time. It's important to note he also had a little bit of a mischievous crush on Bobbie's mother as well. She was described as being a complete sweetheart. At that age, when you encounter a much older woman you find attractive, it's more like one is enamored by the individual as opposed to actually having an attraction. Maybe they are really one in the same. Personally, I can't really attest to having had such feelings at that age, but they would definitely show themselves at later points in my life. Everybody loves a good MILF.

Eventually, Nicos felt as though Bobbie's father was making spiteful comments regarding why he was frequenting their residence. He doesn't know for sure if her father's remarks were racially driven, but his intuition tells him they were. It's so hard to be accurate when we don't ask pertinent questions, so we often use our instincts to dictate our perceptions. Body language and tone become central to how we interpret information. We've all been there, regardless of the context behind said situations.

Because of the actions of Bobbie's father, Nicos started to feel as though things were getting strange. Very uncomfortable and unwelcoming. Neither of those feelings should have been present, as nothing out of line was occurring, but maybe when you deal with fathers, certain irrational elements begin to set in. I'm just playing devil's advocate while in the midst of meticulous analysis. Nonetheless, Nicos and Bobbie both began to pull back from whatever bond was brewing between the two of them. Maybe unfettered racial microaggressions were enough to kill the whole thing. Maybe it was simply because Nicos was a male who was infringing upon his daughter. Maybe a bit of both. Was it possible that the fear of the unknown was the primary issue at hand? In some instances, if one isn't used to being around a certain subgroup of individuals, it can create an awkward disposition within. Regardless, his instinct was that it was all racially driven. It's sad when friendships come to an end because of frivolous external factors.

42

Nicos's shift to middle school was rampant with states of confusion. Partly due to the fact that his mother decided it would be best for him to relocate from Hampton back to Northern Virginia. She was forging ahead with a marriage to a man named Andre and felt as though the environment was stable enough for him to come back. Not back to the Alexandria area, but to Stafford, which was the same town I was living in.

While situations in Hampton had been getting more difficult socially, he ended up being very content with his mother's decision to move him to Stafford. According to Nicos, Hampton wasn't a place he'd ever want to raise children. Although he had a great time there as a kid, his overall perspective of the city was a bit bleak. One would think that with the large-scale military presence in the area, the notion of diversity and inclusion would be prominent. In his section of town, this hadn't been the case at all. He'd begun to wonder why the majority of his neighborhood friends only had other White friends. He was low-key seeking a more diverse peer group. More kids from different backgrounds and nonidentical ethnic groups. At the time, it wasn't going to happen in Hampton. His early exposure to an all-Black private school and then abrupt displacement into a mostly White public school left him longing for a level of inclusion he wasn't going to receive in Southeastern Virginia.

Stafford is about an hour south of Alexandria and far more on the rural side. It was equipped with one main road and maybe two shopping centers at that time. We did have our obligatory Walmart, as would be expected in such a town. The neighborhoods were mostly middle class, with a few small trailer parks spaced out in-between everything. On the outskirts of the middle-class developments were pockets of upper-middle-class developments or even ones that contained homes catered to the wealthy. The area had grown so much since my family moved there four years prior.

Upon moving to Stafford, Andre was now Nicos's father figure. Certainly not in a traditional sense, but a father figure nonetheless. It's definitely not uncommon for kids to have a stepfather. Not quite like his grandfather, who was so much older in age. Andre would become more relatable on some levels. I'm not implying John wasn't relatable to him, but age differences can mean a lot.

He was at a juncture where he didn't feel the need to capitulate to anyone or any particular group. Nicos generally liked everyone and wanted to be able to fit into any group he felt appealed to him, free of any judgments. From an anecdotal point of view, it seems that this is a reality for so many children. Knowledge of self can be so fleeting at this age. Every little struggle can become magnified, as one's maturity isn't typically quite ready to deal with the realities life presents. Small problems become astronomical, and large issues become catastrophic. While this was the case, outwardly exhibiting any misunderstanding was not something he was going to show quite as much. His self-awareness was heightening and becoming paramount to visceral emotions. He kept his feelings within and dealt with them internally. This method greatly diverted from how he handled certain moods during his time as a younger child. Sometimes, significant change can be impactful in terms of our growth. For him, it was satisfactory to have disordered passions on the inside but expressing them on the outside was no longer an option.

Internal struggles were something he and I continued to share, albeit without knowing one another. I feel that in the Black community it's a bit taboo for boys to let their loved ones know that they might be fraught with anything from an emotional perspective. I never knew any men to outwardly speak about the subject matter. Even when interacting with my extended family, our feelings on deep issues were never discussed. Everything else seemed to be fair game. Sports, music, general entertainment, etc. Even the occasional mention of a girl was acceptable. But not any of the sentiments that boiled at our core. I'm not blaming anyone, as this was the status quo, but merely analyzing the effects its absence can produce. Nicos was dealing with a scenario where he knew his mother well but hadn't been living with her, and he didn't know his father at all.

43

In retrospect, it seems like *my* father would have HAD to have been going through *at least* minor mental turmoil when I entered these comparable years. The dude would get up at 5:30 a.m., drive to the Pentagon, work all day, fight gridlock traffic to get home, and then have to deal with some slightly ungrateful kids and the mere existence of a wife. I wouldn't want to deal with that for a single day, let alone *every* day for a multitude of years. It wasn't like we, as kids, were just some bitchy spoiled brats. We really didn't know much about what was going on with him or the macro situations within our family. We were very aloof from the entire process. Terry never mentioned it, so maybe he was cool with the process. His actions said otherwise, and his behavior exuded frustration. But, like I said, I can't be certain. I wish he would have discussed his feelings with me. It would have certainly been hard, and awkward, but probably fruitful. Terry and I took so many tennis-oriented trips together and conversed about some of the most frivolous topics on a regular basis. He and I traveled all over Virginia; Maryland; Washington, DC; and the northern part of North Carolina. We even flew to a few national events in Birmingham, Alabama, and Miami, Florida. These getaways weren't always comfortable. We bickered at times, usually over trivial matters. Whenever he'd become angry, his go-to was to refer to me as being a prima donna. This was a bit odd, because I always felt like the term was slightly endearing. But maybe that's my pompous side speaking. Bougie might even be a more fitting term. There were so many missed opportunities as I look back on it all. Reflection regarding some of our closest relationships can be a motherfucker.

Nicos did have a mother he could reach out to in times of need but wasn't likely to utilize her as a resource unless he felt something was pressing. Appearing to have everything together is important to young boys, especially young boys of color. It's a stigma that runs centuries deep. Unlike myself who had a family dynamic that *appeared* to be stable on its face, his was in a slight state of upheaval.

Long gone were the days of protruding amounts of anger. Maybe he was adjusting to situational circumstances. Learning to cope. He had gone from being an individual who felt the need to conform to someone who was beginning to feel more personal sovereignty. He was at a point where life really had to mean something. It had to carry with it some significant merit. Oftentimes, lesser amounts of care within a given scenario can manifest in the most profound manner. Sometimes situations can be simultaneously vulnerable and fruitful. A blend of despair and repair. Living couldn't just exist in a vacuum any longer. I wished I had taken this step for myself, but I wasn't ready.

Nicos's increasingly enfranchising feeling of autonomy was reflective in his daily actions. Nothing was ever perfect, but he was finding some balance and approaching a level of homeostasis, even during an imperfect period. His more relaxed state served him well in terms of it meshing effortlessly into his middle-school social scene. Dissimilar to myself, who kept my budding but unhurried confidence under wraps, Nicos let his illuminate. He gravitated to a peer group that embodied shared personality traits, as would be the case with most individuals. A group of students whose personalities bounced well off of one another. A healthy intertwinement of boys and girls from an assortment of backgrounds. A conglomerate of kids that would see some of its members form unbreakable ties to one another.

Without mincing words, these were the popular students of their grade, and they mixed with the popular kinds from surrounding grades. A cool crew, equipped with the typical confidence, socialization, love, care, and vanity one would typically associate with such a collection of youths. Nothing at all like the people who I regularly associated with.

Despite the differences between our friends and associates, Nicos and I were cut from a similar cloth. Not an identical cloth, but an analogous one. Both of us spent a significant amount of time living in suburbia as African American preteens and both of us dealt with struggles in terms of fitting in. We had been raised differently, and our family lives were not remotely comparable. If I analyze the two of us from my teenage vantage point, I'd say we were both part of that third category of African Americans that was discussed earlier. Neither of us were *trying* to be anything we weren't. We weren't cultured to feel as though our race defined who we were, nor was it conveyed to us that it was something to run from. We didn't fit into the boxes the world would have generally liked to have placed us in. In my opinion, the sum of our parts had seemingly caused him and me to express ourselves in a manner that would have been described as contrary to the norm.

I feel like we both exuded a budding type of masculinity, but our communication of said trait was dissimilar. I basically said very little and let my actions do the talking. One of my goals, for better or for worse, was always to let my nonchalant attitude speak for itself (which actually may have led people to assume I acted more on the feminine side). Nicos's demeanor was a bit more demonstrative. Maybe our differences were directly related to the presence, or lack thereof, of an integral father figure. Although my dad was a staple in my life, he and I were consistently engaging in very minor conflicts, mainly rooted in our emotional dispositions being very unalike. With Nicos not having his father in his life (while being raised by grandparents and a single mother), a slight chip on his shoulder could have been developed, causing more of a bold disposition. I know for a fact that I established one (the chip on the shoulder), but it's because I held so much inside for so long without a sufficient outlet.

44

Between Nicos's eighth and ninth grade years, he developed rich friendships with two students in particular. One with an African American kid named Jared, and another with a White girl named Ashely. Both relationships were based on completely different premises but were rooted in foundations that were awfully sturdy. Bonds that were equipped to withstand the test of time.

Ashley was one of the first people Nicos met upon moving to Stafford. She could be described as one of his ride-or-die friends. Always by one another's side and around to comfort in times of need. She was an athletic girl whose skill set was very concentrated within the discipline of dance (it's always nice to have ladies like that around). Their relationship would seem to be pretty surface level, but it did get deeper at times. Just as important as his relationship with Ashley was that of his fondness for her parents. They were almost like a second family to him. He really relished being looked at as one of them. The general camaraderie and togetherness invoked an inviting feeling. Ashley became the type of friend Nicos would do anything for. Despite her being an attractive and intelligent girl and him being considered to be a handsome boy, nothing ever happened between the two of them in a romantic sense. Their bond was strictly platonic and both of them are better for it now. She was an exceptional and beneficial friend for him to have upon arriving in a new locale.

His friendship with Jared started with Nicos and a few other boys walking around the St. George's Estates neighborhood. Jared's mother noticed the kids heading to the basketball court and encouraged her son to join them. He agreed and it immediately became clear they were all the same age. According to Nicos, Jared was far more skilled and schooled them like crazy. It was a total shitshow. A very *White Men Can't Jump* situation. Eventually the boys laughed off Jared's dominant performance and he and Nicos forged a solid friendship. As two teenage Black boys growing up in Stafford County, they had a lot in common. Both had gregarious and outgoing personalities. They mutually felt the need to go after the prettiest girls and one-up each other in a tongue-in-cheek manner. Obviously one could surmise that this type of continuous interaction could lead to some conflict, which is definitely true, but it was all chalked up to healthy competition. Being minorities, they developed the need to stick together. Once again, a friendship that would stand the test of time and become extremely beneficial upon Nicos moving to Stafford. These were the types of ironclad connections I wished I had forged during that time in my life. For him, they definitely led to a domino effect in terms of embracing new friendships that carved out a stable place for him entering the ninth grade. A stupendous position for him to grow within.

45

That was Nicos in a nutshell, up until the early stages of high school. So much of who he was at that point was based on how he was cultured. One can clearly see that growing up Black in suburbia is quite a tricky task. This was especially true during the '80s and '90s, as the country was going through some significant social changes. Things were certainly better than they had been in past generations, but the general adult public was reeling from a time that was riddled with disconnect and rampant with stereotypes. The children were the collateral damage. Living through it all was sort of like having to do cultural gymnastics on a regular basis. At one point, something very specific is expected of you, and then it can all change at the drop of a hat. Issues dealing with family also throw a bit of a monkey wrench into any situation. Personally, I can't imagine what it would have been like to grow up without a father, as my father's involvement was paramount to so much of what I achieved. Clearly it isn't something one *has* to have, but it can definitely help. It could also hurt, depending on the type of father we're talking about.

Nicos's mother went above and beyond in order to assist in playing a role that was rooted in duality. Having to morph into what a mother and a father might have to be, depending on the situation. In addition, changing relationship dynamics with one's parents can also be an excruciating life factor to have to wrestle with.

His mother and grandparents did such a remarkable job raising him. I can't say enough about how commendable their efforts were, and a major part of that is a testament to how long I've known some of them, even if general contact has been spotty. Earlier in this piece, I mentioned an excerpt from the theme song to the late 1970s and '80s television show *The Facts of Life*. The words in that song ring so true to all of us. It's so distinct with respect to the individualistic elements that humans can encompass.

The influences that music, film, and comics had on Nicos really placed him in a unique space. Little pieces shoved into a blender that would come out constructively. Sometimes life brings you back and forth so much that you get used to being jerked around. But in the process, our outlets, no matter what they are, can aid in bringing us balance. For Nicos, his family and close friends gave him a solid support system. That same type of human sustenance wouldn't have worked for me, as I was cultured a bit differently and wouldn't have been used to it. So much of what I wrestled with was handled in slight isolation. Even if from an outsider's perspective, it appeared as though I had a vast support system. This was not the case in terms of its sincere reality. Nuances can alter so much in terms of who we are. What was fruitful for him might not have been beneficial for me. And that's completely alright. It's important to note that moving forward into the third phase of this piece, I didn't really know Nicos particularly well at its starting point. At least not in terms of us being friends. High school was entirely new territory. A brand-new horizon.

PHASE 3

46

The latter stages of high school proved to be pivotal times for me. Honestly, it's probably that way for most kids. It seems like so much of what you have to deal with is filled with rites of passages. One foot is still immersed in being a child and the other is approaching adulthood. So many new experiences with regards to education, interpersonal situations, sexuality, aesthetics, extracurricular activity, etc. I was a real dork but an athletic dork. A really successful athletic dork, to be more specific. But I was clearly struggling to find myself in so many ways. My sense of style was certainly unique, and at the time it embodied who I was. But it was pretty lame. I was obsessed with fitted shirts and slightly baggy cargo pants. Maybe using the term "fitted" is a bit of an understatement. My shirts were tight. Too tight. In hindsight, I was trying to show off my athletic physique, but it really wasn't the best look. I was definitely doing too much, and I'm not remotely ashamed to admit it.

I was a really smart kid but not quite as smart as some of my peers. After being admitted into the Commonwealth Governor's School program, I was consistently surrounded by brilliant individuals. My strengths were in English and history. Math and science were my weak disciplines. Some of my classmates were very strong in all areas, which once again placed me in the middle of academia, as I saw it. This wasn't really that big of a deal, but it did place me in an envious predicament. I was amazed by the type of people who could write a dissertation on the historical impact of Frederick Douglass, balance scientific equations, and succeed in a course like trigonometry. There was no way *I* could excel in such a manner across the board.

My excellence in the tennis world set me apart from my classmates and provided a lot of recognition and opportunity. But even as a successful athlete, I was a big fish in a small pond. I won district titles and competed in the Virginia State high school tournament on two occasions. I was the number-one seed all throughout high school and obtained a top-thirty ranking in the Mid-Atlantic region of the United States.

All of this was amazing, but the minute I stepped out of my bubble and played in a national event, I got my ass kicked, royally. I was an accomplished middle-of-the-road type player. Strong, but I didn't have enough size, height, or focus. I also wasn't really the type of player that was groomed to play from a young age. That may sound like a ridiculous piece of analysis, but in a sport like tennis, it matters. Most elite tennis players begin playing at the age of five or six, and hire select coaches to guide their development. My father and I kind of went into it all in a bit of a blind manner. I started playing at age nine very casually. It was a hobby for me, rather than a sport that was intended to be a meal ticket. I really didn't take it all super seriously until I was about fourteen, which was far too late. Winning didn't make me feel like I was on top of the world, and losing didn't tear me up inside. With an attitude like that, you'll never become an elite champion, unless your physical gifts are uncanny. I was certainly no freak athlete.

Tennis is a very expensive sport to excel at. The rackets, strings, shoes, clothing, lessons, and tournament costs could run someone a monthly bill of over $2,000, and that might even be on the low end. Not only did I start playing the sport a bit late in age, but as a family we didn't have the resources to get me caught up with the best players. Looking back, I don't really think I had the desire either. As a team (my father and I), we did a great job, but just not great enough. And in the end, that's okay. If playing the sport did anything for me, it aided in my development in ways that would not have been obtained otherwise. It helped give me a sense of self, continued with my attention to physical fitness, helped solidify my budding confidence, and provided some much-needed mental serenity. Actually, colleges even began to contact me for opportunities within higher education, but those letters generally fell on deaf ears.

I had friends, but as I stated earlier, nobody whom I could really relate to on a non-surface level. Nothing with any significant amount of depth. My first noteworthy female friend during this period was a girl named Amber. She was half-Indian and half-White, so I'd imagine that she felt placed in the middle a lot as well. I will note again that I didn't feel displaced exclusively because of my ethnicity but more because of how the element of nurture affected my persona. This wasn't something she and I ever talked about in detail. Amber was also part of the Governor's School program, so we were both intelligent individuals. She's actually one of the smartest people I've ever met. This factor was part of what ended up being the demise of our close friendship. I don't think our brains really matched in a completely cohesive manner during those years. It was like we were an open circuit that decided to close when it felt like it. We definitely weren't connecting consistently enough to sustain anything substantial.

My sense of humor was developing into something that was pretty off-kilter, and hers was a bit more typical. I'd make fun of people who were in the Governor's School program. Calling them "nerds" or "dweebs" in a facetious manner (probably as a defense mechanism), and she'd take offense to that. This was frustrating but was also healthy to realize that not everyone is for everybody. It's also important to acknowledge that the phrase "wrong place, wrong time" has some significant merit. All things considered, this friendship was the closest that I'd come to finding a platonic equal. Something that was nearing the precipice of my social yearnings. In hindsight, I will say that I have some regrets with respect to my friendship with her. It's okay to admit that one is sorry for their actions, or for not letting a joke die, as opposed to having it proliferate for your benefit. But this is all a part of maturing. It's all a part of us becoming something we find favorable within ourselves. Even when we fall short, it's the unceasing effort that is key.

My demeanor around girls continued to be awkward. My demeanor around most people was awkward. This is probably because I was continuously searching for something and never quite finding it. Not in myself and certainly not with others. It didn't help that most of my Governor's School peers were also fairly awkward. It was like we all had a little bit of "prodigy" in us, on some level. Each of us had some acute knowledge about something or an interest that would set us apart from the fray. Social development was a bit stagnant. Like I said much earlier, so much was done to help with growth on the outside for me, but little was being done to develop the mental health side. Not in terms of what was going on at school, on the tennis court, or at home. The person inside was stunted, growth wise. And so much of this was based on the lack of mental cultivation by my parents. People thought I was cool, I guess, but I think it was because I was trying. I was "putting on." It certainly wasn't effortless. I tried to act like it was, but it wasn't at all. It wouldn't be until I entered adulthood that my effortless vibes would become synonymous with my persona. I did begin to really appreciate the fact that I had been exposed to such diverse elements throughout my life. Although the process was grating, it served me well in many ways. My overall openness and general relatability made me seem pretty accessible. Even if it wasn't the legitimate case at the time, it seemed that way.

47

On the flip side of my development during high school, was that of Nicos's. He and I were like night and day during these years, yet so similar, and this is being said in hindsight. I feel like so many of the Black students living in suburban Northern Virginia at that time dealt with comparable internal struggles. Nicos's overall vibes were far more straightforward than mine. He obtained lifelong friends at a young age. He made himself appealing with the popular high school brass. He seemed to fit in, even when he really didn't. He had a much easier time inter-acting with girls in comparison to myself. I wasn't super aware of him, but I was aware enough, I guess. I had heard the name floating around. But honestly, I was too much in my own head and my own situations to really give a shit about names that were just floating around. This was, of course, unless the names impacted my personal well-being. Contrary to that sentiment, most of the Black students at North Stafford really did know of one another. I'm not saying it's innate or anything, but maybe more like "game recognize game." We all knew who was making noise. We knew who was getting the girls. We knew which students were performing well in the athletic arena. We knew which students were academically successful. Maybe being marginalized caused us all to become more aware of what was going on amongst us.

I stayed in my bubble. It was filled with smart kids and great athletes. This was something I really needed to break out of but wasn't aware. Nicos walked around with his head held high. I did the same but not with a similar amount of bravado. I was always on edge, where he didn't *seem* to be. These are all points of analysis from an optics perspective, as I really didn't know him at all. I was, however, becoming closer with some of the members of his graduating class, which was one year beneath mine. I seemed to relate better to them. I was a part of the class of 2001, whereas he was in the 2002 group. For some reason, that one year made a huge difference to me. My class was divided. Literally, it was very black and white, from a social perspective. People stayed within their predisposed boxes. Nicos's class was far more diverse. I knew this before ever coming into contact with him. It was obviously from an optics perspective. Certain cliques from the class of 2002 were far more likely to include individuals from different ethnic groups and backgrounds.

I had developed friendships with members of his class through playing tennis. One of which was my doubles partner, Zach, who ended up becoming a bit of an unknowing liaison between Nicos and I. Zach was well beyond his years in terms of coolness and charisma. He was almost like a slightly heavier version of Nick Carter from the Backstreet Boys. The kind of dude that would casually hit on a forty-year old waitress while being at the ripe age of sixteen. He'd do it just to do it. For fun and maybe to cause a minor scene. Always in good spirits and constantly ready to get wild. A real party-animal type kid but with a good heart. Zach had an amazing family by his side. His mother was always super sweet and kindhearted to me. He's actually one of the most enigmatic people I've ever met. At the time, I think we gravitated toward one another because we were so different. A major commonality between us was our sense of humor. We could joke about anything without being offended. At times, his actions would get a bit outlandish, and I'd have to reel him in.

Sometimes he and I would have practice sessions on a Friday and then hit the mall afterward. Most of the time we didn't even purchase anything. Just walked around for the scenery, maybe just to look at girls and dabble in some light dialogue. Engaging with random people was way more his thing than mine. We usually stuck around the area, but on occasion we'd go up north to Alexandria or Woodbridge. Both of our graduating classes liked to party, but my friendships with individuals in his class were developing quickly. Their gatherings were more my style. Maybe that's another ode to their heightened level of diversity. It was a factor that really aided in making things more comfortable for me.

Zach was really good friends with Nicos. He would share stories about random shit that would happen within their circles, usually during our tennis sessions. Looking back on it, he probably shared too much. I was always a bit envious, as their lives seemed far more exciting than mine. My life was full of schoolwork and sports. Most of the time it felt like I couldn't get out from underneath either of the two entities. The second I was caught up with my studies, I had to go out of town for a weekend tennis tournament. Maybe it would have all been easier if I were winning at an elite level. I don't really know. But what I do know is that it was both frustrating and exhausting. My stress level was through the roof. I felt like I could never catch up. From the outside looking in, Nicos's social life appeared to be full of parties, sexual activity, and booze. Even when the stuff I heard wasn't sexual in nature, it still sounded like it was. Zach was unquestionably romanticizing his accounts. From the tales he told, either someone's parents were always out of town, or they were chill enough to host their offspring and company. Although much of what was shared may not have been 100 percent accurate, they came off as appealing, and that's all I really cared about.

Adding to what they were doing as a crew, they had connections to groups of girls that were younger than them. This was an intriguing factor, as it pretty much guaranteed an excessive supply of ladies for the guys. I don't mean this to downgrade or impugn the young girls, but this is a factual point of analysis when it comes to the minds of young boys. These girls got around. And they did it in a fairly unapologetic fashion. From a candid perspective, I was quite jealous. I've said it before and I'll say it again: these years are tough when it comes to dealing with sexuality. It's so hard to contextualize how to behave in potential sexual encounters.

Not only were these young ladies serving it up on a silver platter, but they looked good in the process. I don't mean in the act but just their overall vibe. They really knew how to flaunt themselves. Product placement can be everything, and that's how I viewed them at the time. That probably comes off as demeaning, but I'm just being honest regarding my teenage perspective. The envy was real. Very real. But I sat back and lived vicariously through the stories Zach told. It was rare that what he shared dealt with very explicit situations. They usually included light petting or making out. The latter was always a given. Every now and again, someone would get fingered, or maybe oral sex would be included. Regardless, it was all fairly racy to me, as I wasn't getting any at all.

Whenever I'd hang out with a girl, the evening would usually end with me being "friend zoned." It was super lame. I think that at the time, I was super lame, mainly when hanging around girls. There was a large part of me that wished I would be invited to some random gathering and one of the younger girls would just put it on me. I mean, stranger things have certainly happened. It isn't like this would have been incomprehensible, given that I was a notable high school athlete and all. I was confused, and I was doing too much. Trying too hard. Posturing when it wasn't necessary. It was an awfully puzzling time for me as a young adult. It's not as if my situation was completely unique. I feel like most teenagers are clueless during these years, but it doesn't alter the words that pour onto these pages. These are tough times, and the more stories that are told, the better the setup can be for generations to come.

48

Time went on, as it had to. My life continued on the same trajectory. Weeks were filled with school and tennis practices. Weekends were typically devoted to tournament play and then back to the grind on Monday. Tennis is a different type of sport because it doesn't really have seasons of competition. The events occur all year and typically on the weekends. If you don't compete in events regularly, your ranking will inevitably fall, and most kids want to avoid that. Now, there is a high school season, which is typically in the spring, but that's completely outside of regional play. The most elite players don't even engage in high school competition, as it can be seen as a waste of time. Do you think that Rafael Nadal or Roger Federer were worried about high school tennis? Nah.

Whenever my weekends weren't filled with athletic competition, I felt very free. That was when I'd find time to go out. Experience life as a more typical teenager. Nothing too crazy but just general socialization. On one of these more free weekends, Zach and I went to a Mexican restaurant in Woodbridge. It was a good time, as it always was, but something was a bit different on this occasion. Our conversations were typically frivolous. Centering on our lives as high school athletes and whatever was going on within his social clique. Not really so much about me, as I guess I seemed too tame. I'm probably being overly modest in my description. Maybe I wasn't really THAT tame, but my social insecurities led me to believe that I was. My confidence level was high, internally, but not outwardly high enough for me to project anything particularly interesting about my own life. Living vicariously through others felt more appropriate than delving into whatever was going on within myself.

On this day in particular, our interaction turned a bit more candid. Zach began to probe a little deeper, asking questions about my preferences in relationships. Things like: did I want to date? Did I have a current crush on anyone? Did I have any ethnic or racial preferences? Would I be interested in seeing someone who was a bit younger than myself? I was definitely thrown off a bit, but I chalked it up to friends having a simple discussion. I mean, as relationships develop, one would assume the depths of conversation would become more personal, right? There was something different about this moment though. It was almost as if Zach was asking for another reason. Like he had an ulterior motive or prior knowledge about something. Whatever the case was, I knew it would come out eventually. And if it was nothing, that would reveal itself as well. Everything would be whatever it would be. On the way home, we stopped at Best Buy. For some reason, I wanted to pick up the newest Cypress Hill album. I didn't even listen to Cypress Hill like that, but I thought it would be cool to act like I did. Doing too much once again. Interestingly enough, I was into far more edgy acts, but in that moment, my gut said to buy that particular record. Random events on a typical evening. It left me with a lot to question. So goes life as a teenager. There was so much happening. So many factors to digest. But per usual, Monday came too soon.

49

Two-thirty p.m., after what was a typical day. I was just leaving my seventh-period human physiology class. It was a nice spring day, and there was always something comforting about leaving school on an afternoon like that. For whatever reason, tennis practice had been canceled, which contributed to a mild sense of euphoria for me. I went to my locker to grab my belongings and was shocked to see a note lodged in between the small openings.

Hi Justin,

Just wanted you to know that I've been watching you around school and I think you're really cute. Would you be interested in getting together sometime? I hope so!

XOXO,

Savannah

Initially, I was taken aback by such a note. It was the first time that I'd received something so forward. It was such a brash move. My mind was moving like an active pinball machine. Did Zach know about this all along? Was this why he had asked me all of those probing questions at dinner? If so, why not just come out and talk to me about it at face value? I was excited but then thought about who the note was actually from. It took me a minute to process it all, but after some time, I gathered myself.

Savannah? Savannah Miller? She was maybe two years younger than me. A track athlete. Popular in her class. I thought she was good looking but nothing super special or unique. Certainly not unique enough to jump at the opportunity to be in her company. That might sound a little pompous, but the mind of an eleventh grader is full of all sorts of shit and pretty preoccupied. Some of it may sound condescending and selfish. It was common for guys to get shit for messing with younger girls but mainly from other girls that were in the same class as the guys. It seemed like a jealousy thing. Savannah shot her shot, which was cool and very flattering, but not something that I really thought I had time to entertain. I did feel a bit compelled to respond though. The fact that it was written as a note meant I would have to reach out to her in order to provide an answer. I was prepared to let it go, even though it was partially what I had been seeking all along. Someone else to be the aggressor and aid in alleviating my trepidations. Someone to do the hard lifting for me. Maybe even someone to initiate the type of sexual activity I had been exposed to via pornography and all of the explicit stories I'd heard. Since I didn't have to be the initiator, I might come off as far less awkward. All things considered, I was still willing to let the situation pass me by.

I let it all marinate for a few days without sharing anything with my Governor's School friends. Savannah was a younger outsider, so they wouldn't have known much about her anyway. When I was at my base school of North Stafford High, people began to approach me, as if they had known about the note. They appeared to be curious. It seemed as though every few hours someone would come up to me saying something like, "Hey man, I heard Savannah likes you. What are you going to do?" This bombardment of questions had me really analyzing the situation further. I began to weigh my options, especially from a social standpoint. Peer pressure was a monster. So many random people were in my ear. Some of them were students I wasn't even familiar with. My perspective on the issue was beginning to shift.

All of a sudden, Savannah went from being not very unique to being quite sexy. In all honesty, she actually was pretty good looking, I guess. I had been downplaying that aspect in my own head on purpose. Sometimes it can be difficult to really decipher what one thinks is appealing at such a young age. You know what you like but are still a bit "wet behind the ears" in terms of the development of one's taste. Outside pressures can shape what you find pleasing, and I was definitely affected by them. Personally, I've always had a thing for curvy women with a bit more meat on their bones, but the desire to conform typically guided me in a different direction. Teenage years are rough, and the ability to stand up for what *you* actually want isn't easy.

There was a mysterious level of projection that Savannah's eyes conveyed. As I thought about things more, appealing qualities seemed to be popping up by the minute. Her eyes were a bit evil looking. That may sound pejorative on its face, but I liked that about her. I've always had a thing for wicked-looking eyes and still do. That particular feature would usually lead me to be physically intrigued. Maybe "cat eyes" is a more appropriate way to describe them, from an aesthetic point of view. Certainly feline looking. The type of eyes you don't want to look directly into but you do it anyway because the overall lure is too enticing to turn away from. Such a seductive piece of her demeanor.

Her involvement in track assured that she was physically fit. Her body was appealing to me. Curvy and a bit voluptuous for her age. Not skinny but athletic. Muscular thighs. Fairly thin waist. Developed calf muscles. A major focal point of her figure was her breasts. They were disproportionately large compared to the rest of her. I've never been much of a breast guy, but when you're a teenager, you often just go with what you think would be generally appealing. Whenever my father and I would go shopping for magazines, I noticed so many men's publications focusing on marketing women who had hefty breasts. They were in my face all of the time. These minor pieces of influence sometimes skew our perspectives enough to the point where we go against what we would have naturally thought or done. I suppose that can be chalked up to effective advertising. Not so much peer pressure but definitely a significantly impactful medium for sure.

Savannah had a bronze skin tone, but she was White. Dark brown hair and dark-ish features. Almost Brazilian looking. A sly grin that was devious. Her demeanor screamed of something seeking acceptance. Sometimes it seemed to me that she was playing dumb, but that was just her disposition. She wasn't particularly well spoken and often stumbled over her words. Not because of a speech impediment but more out of confusion in terms of what to say. When this would happen, she'd usually look in another direction. Her eyes would wander. Savannah definitely did not have a poker face. Maybe she was just very nervous. That particular element was a paradox for me with respect to girls I had grown accustomed to being around as a part of the Governor's School program. Those young ladies were so well spoken and were always "on." So professional, even in class. Savannah was anything but that. I didn't mind. The more I mulled over everything, the nicer she became to look at.

50

Regardless of everything, I still found myself slowly coming around to the idea of giving her a chance. There was something enticing there, and temptation is a hell of a drug. She would come by my locker on a daily basis just to say hello. That was a first for me. The more she paid her visits, the more apparent it was to me that I found her scent to be alluring. It was something I got used to, and I enjoyed it. An inviting fragrance will always do it for me. Up until this point, no girl had gotten close enough to me to really dissect their aroma. I'm not sure if it was her shampoo, perfume, lotion, or all of it intertwined into a lovely concoction, but it was pleasant. Sweet and sultry. Blending bits of honey and lemon. Slightly jasmine, maybe. Certainly distinctive.

Her persistence was appealing, and I eventually caved. It wasn't like my arm had to be twisted super harshly or anything. I mean, what did I really have to lose, right? I figured it was a situation that needed to be explored. Even the worst-case scenario could allow for some growth, or at least some fun. This was something I really needed to entertain, so I decided to move forward. Game on. I asked her out, even though I really didn't know what that entailed at the time. Would we have to go on a formal date? I'd been out with girls before but never with someone who had made their affection so vocal. The last time a girl was so forward was that one German girl from the charter bus in kindergarten.

Anyhow, Savannah obliged, and we met up at a local McDonald's after school one day. The spot was only about a two-minute walk from the school parking lot. I offered to give her a ride, but she insisted she was okay with walking. She had a few friends with her, so maybe it would give them an opportunity to do a bit of gossiping prior to her and I meeting up. Just a bit of mild speculation on my end.

We ended up having a pretty good time. I wasn't particularly nervous, which was a bit surprising to me. Given everything surrounding the situation, it was definitely a date, albeit an informal one. She laughed a lot, and I talked a lot. I guess I had a lot to say. Even if she was humoring me, I didn't care. I was going with the flow. It was the overall experience that was most pertinent. We each finished a small meal, and then I took her home, which was about ten minutes away. When we arrived at her house, I was surprised that nobody was home. This was around four in the afternoon. Whenever I'd visit with a friend after school, there was always a parent home. Or at least a sibling or two. Not in this case though.

Savannah was a true latchkey kid in the realest sense of the term. She was being raised solely by her mother. I actually don't even recall her ever speaking about her dad. If you're not familiar with the "latchkey" term, it basically means a child is home without adult supervision for some part of the day. I didn't go inside her house. We just sat on her porch and talked. It was comforting. Even though it was our first time really hanging out, we seemed to enjoy one another's company. The sun began to set, and it was about time for me to be leaving. It was maybe seven in the evening, and her mother still wasn't home. The lingering question on my mind was whether or not I should give her a goodbye kiss. This caused me to prolong my departure, but ultimately I decided not to. I definitely chickened out, as that would have been my first real kiss. I opted for a hug instead.

My actions were frustrating to me. My eyes rolled as I turned away from her. She seemed disappointed as well, but I imagine that a far less desirable outcome would have ensued had I tried to kiss her. It would have been awkward as hell. I'm pretty positive it would have been obvious that I didn't know what I was doing. I wasn't willing to take that type of risk. But all in all, it was a fun time. Definitely a respectable initial outing.

51

Savannah and I hung out like this for about a month. I'd go over to her house after tennis practice maybe three or four days out of the week. Mostly sitting on the couch watching television together. Sometimes cuddled up, but usually about a foot apart from one another. There really wasn't any significant affection being shown at all between the two of us. If I were to gauge the situation based on the scenarios Zach had shared with me, things had gone on for too long for us not to have shared any intimate moments. I wasn't going to force anything, but I kind of hoped maybe she would. This was all magnified since we had so much alone time. Seemingly far more than a couple of teenagers should have. So many of my peers would have been chomping at the bit to be in my situation. And these weren't even moments when a parent might consciously choose to give a kid their space. This was just their status quo. There can be so many bumps in the road for a teenager while they struggle with aspects of sexuality. One minute you're charged with confidence and then, in the blink of an eye, your insecurities start to show.

On one occasion, I did run into her mother. She had gotten home early from work one day. I was introduced and we chatted for a brief moment. No significant questions were asked, which was a bit unexpected, seeing as how I was a slightly older boy hanging out with her daughter. She was a nice lady but didn't seem remotely protective or even nurturing. I think she had her own shit going on and wasn't very concerned with me.

I ended up becoming acquaintances with her brother and older sister as well. I probably should have thought about formally asking Savanah to be my girlfriend, but I was just taking things one day at a time. Our conversations were cool but not particularly insightful. Not very much depth. Most of what we talked about was all surface-level type stuff. I started to wonder if I was doing all of this because it was perceived as the "thing to do" rather than something I was actually really invested in. After all, I should have been invested in it, right? When a pretty young lady is actively trying to be with you, you're supposed to be fully engaged, aren't you? My brain was full of uncertainty and contradictions. So many lingering queries.

Although I was seriously starting to question this association with Savannah, we never really deliberated over anything involving the two of us. It was probably a topic we weren't ready to broach, possibly out of fear. I could sense that things might be getting to the point of redundancy. Maybe it was becoming stagnant. I still hadn't made the move to make us "official" in terms of being boyfriend and girlfriend. She appeared to be frustrated while I was just confused. As I mentioned, some of our couch hangouts did involve cuddling. A bit of light touching. But I feel like she was seeking something with more significance. Not necessarily from a commitment standpoint but from a physical one. After all, it was commonplace for teens with some alone time to do a bit of casual exploration, which doesn't explicitly *have* to imply sex. But it doesn't negate the possibility either. I really wasn't ready for all of that, but it wasn't something I could be vocal about. Certainly not without seeming like a punk bitch or a pansy.

I had no idea how to proceed, so I just kept it all moving at the snail's pace I had grown accustomed to. Although I was at a loss in what had become a slightly casual relationship, my social standing had garnered some significant enhancement. This boost was recognized by a lot of the upperclassmen, but I started to notice some of the Black girls treating me differently. The predicament was reminiscent of the judgments I had observed my mother and aunt making at the sight of interracial couples in the mall years prior. A few actually approached me and asked if I was seeing "that White girl." In class, some started to treat me as an outcast or a pariah. I played it off like it wasn't bothersome, but internally it played on some of my insecurities, as I was aware of the stereotype. If a Black male made the conscious decision to date a White girl, the instant perception was that he was proverbially saying that Black girls were somehow not good enough.

My actions weren't going to change based on any of this. And even while I didn't agree with their perspectives, I did slightly empathize with them, if I looked at it from their vantage point. Especially from a historical perspective. Despite this being the case, my macro point of view was that their outlook was incorrect. It goes back to the notion of meddling in the affairs of others when said affairs don't concern "you." Savannah being White really didn't matter to me either way. The notion that it mattered to others was just something I was going to have to block out of my mind. I'd have to act like it was a completely nonexistent issue.

52

Obviously, throughout this little minor courting process with Savannah, having a vehicle was an integral factor. At the time, my dad and I shared a car, which worked out pretty well for me. I'm actually kind of surprised he was okay with such an arrangement, seeing as how it benefited myself a bit more than it did him. Maybe I can chalk that up to him wanting to help me out during a pivotal time in my life. The ability to get around is crucial for a teenager, especially once you start dating. Anyhow, he would drive to work with me as the passenger, and then once we arrived at his job, we'd switch seats and I'd take the car back home to pick up my brother. After that, my brother and I would ride to school, where I'd have the car until right after tennis practice. Then, I'd go back to my dad's job, get him, and he would drive us home. It was definitely a lengthy process, but it really helped me learn some responsibility and independence.

One early Sunday morning, I had booked a tennis session with a coach up in the Montclair area. This was roughly a thirty-five minute drive north from our home in Stafford. I left the house at about 7:30 a.m. and went into my parents' bedroom to inquire as to whether or not I should put any gas in the car. My father informed me that the gas light had just come on, but that

I should still be able to get to Montclair and back. He said *he* would put gas in the car the next morning. I must say that Terry was very groggy during our brief chat, but he still said what he said nonetheless. I took his words at face value and did my thing. Everything went as planned. I went to tennis practice and came home that afternoon. When I arrived at the house, I even asked my dad if he wanted me to go back out and get some gas just so he'd be comfortable driving to work. He continued to assure me that things would be fine, so I adhered to his directive.

For whatever reason, I took the bus to school the next day, and my dad drove to and from work on his own. The gas issue was at the back of my mind, knowing that the empty light was still on, but since he told me not to worry about it, I did my best not to concern myself. It was a pretty normal day, and in the early evening, maybe around 5:00 p.m., I was doing what I normally did. At home doing homework and watching *TRL* or *Rap City*. I don't really remember which. Terry abrasively walked in from work and was absolutely livid. Actually, livid would be an understatement to describe his demeanor. He was fuming. Seething. Incensed. Apparently, he was so confident that the car wouldn't run out of gas he didn't fuel up on his way to work. His plan was to fill the tank up on his way home. Well, on his way home, the car ran out of gas on a long rural back road. If I remember correctly, it was on Mountainview Road. Terry had to leave the car in a shallow ditch, walk to the nearest gas station, fill up one of those little red lawn mower–style gas containers, and then walk back to his car to put the gas in. He did this, and then made it home in one piece, but his dissatisfaction with me was glaring. I'd imagine that the embarrassment factor was pretty high for him as well. Walking on the side of the road with a gas can, assuming that his son should have put gas into the tank. Oh well. Shit happens, right? I was sorry but not *that* sorry.

I'd never experienced my dad's anger as much as it portrayed itself in that one moment. He was cursing at me nonstop. I hadn't ever heard my father using profanity before, so this was really weird and a bit scary. Momentarily, I didn't think it was out of the realm of possibility for him to attack me. Once his expletive-laden rant was over, he assured me he was going to take my license away for a few months. I had no choice but to give it to him against my will, but I wasn't going down without a fight.

In my opinion, he was completely in the wrong. He had consciously told me not to put any gas in the car, so I did as I was told. To me, he was way out of line. Even though he was half-asleep, he still said what he said. One could argue that I should have been more aware of the situation and put gas in the car anyway, but shit, I was trying to save my money. I was sixteen. I might have needed cash for a date with Savannah. I thought my argument, in the most literal sense, was far stronger than his. Terry wasn't having it though. Not at all. So, I did the most bitch-ass thing I've ever done in my entire life. I called my mother at work and told her Dad had been cursing me out at will. Given her staunch religious beliefs, I knew she would support me against him using profanity toward a minor. I laid the situation out to her, and of course, I made it seem like I was the more rational individual. I may have even fabricated a few things in order to tip the situation in my favor. This was the first time I had ever attempted to use my mother to be on my side in a disagreement, and it worked.

Later that evening at dinner, my dad came to me with my driver's license and returned it. He said he was sorry and recognized that he should have just asked me to put some gas in the car on my way to tennis practice. I'm not sure if he was just parroting my mother's talking points or if he actually believed what he was saying. Either way, I was the victor, but I still wasn't sure if I had done something wrong by running to my mother. He seemed to be pretty pissed off in the process, but he still carried everything out in a civil manner. In the end, it actually did lead to my dad and I forming a tighter bond, because increased mutual respect was gained. In some strange and twisted sense, I think he admired the fact I used logic to get over and that I wasn't willing to relinquish any ground. I'm pretty sure it was the first time he had ever said sorry to me. Conversely, it was also the first time I had noticed him reacting with such heightened visceral emotion. Definitely a seminal moment for me and maybe for him too. With all of that being said, I had my driver's license in my possession, and I could start seeing Savannah again. I was only out of the game for about a day, so it's not like that part was a huge deal. For all intents and purposes, it was a very emotional situation, but I was back in business. Right then, that's really all that I cared about.

53

While Savannah and I hadn't crossed any boundaries from a sexual standpoint, the general perception from others was that we had. It was a social norm to have done so, and just the impression of us being together created this illusion. This misconception began to take a minor toll on Savannah, as she was starting to force the topic of sex into our conversations. I didn't avoid them, but I wasn't heavily engaged either. This lack of obligatory commitment on my part added to her dissatisfaction, but like I've said, my popularity was skyrocketing.

Previously, I'd enter and exit the school pretty quickly, and I'd either go straight to class or right to my car to leave. It was evident to me that the more social students would hang around the middle of the cafeteria at the end of the day. That's where kids went once they had been vetted and accepted into given cliques. Since I had been seeing Savannah, I was on people's radar for something other than winning tennis matches or being an academic standout. As I'd walk past this section of the school, I noticed other kids beginning to shout me out or sometimes even coming over to greet me. The most satisfying gesture was when I'd be asked to come join the groups in some light socialization.

This was most notable with Zach. My big, bad, braggadocious, doubles partner was suddenly my most vocal champion in terms of ingratiating me with the cool kids. The type of people who I'd never really hung with in social circles. A far cry from my Governor's School comrades, but those students (myself included) were really dope in their own right. It wasn't the most comfortable situation, as you had to move differently when group dynamics began to shift, but I stood back and watched as an observer. A people watcher. A position that would allow me to be simultaneously social and judgmental. I wasn't aware of it at the time, but this was a role I would always come to find appealing.

Upon leaving school for the parking lot one day, Savannah and I walked past a large group of students gathered in the center of the cafeteria. Zach called me over in true Zach fashion. He yelled across the room, "Marlowe!! Get over here, bro!!" It became common for people to refer to me by solely using my last name. I was holding Savanah's hand and lightly tugged on it to motion her to join me in meeting up with Zach and his friends. Maybe that was presumptuous of me. I never like to make assumptions, but this was a knee-jerk reaction. She pulled away, not so much because something was wrong, but because she just didn't have any desire to socialize at that moment.

Savannah opted to take the bus home, and I met with the students in the cafeteria. Most of them were pretty nice, although there was a pervasive streak of arrogance in the room. I wondered if their confident exterior was a veil for something that was burning deeper inside. It seemed like everyone was either attempting to one-up someone else or just content to be part of a slightly trendy social scene. The latter would sit quietly and do their best to blend in. It was an environment full of paradoxes, yet it all meshed together like Jean-Michel Basquiat painting. Facets that wouldn't seem to work well but created an awfully cohesive identity.

It was fairly obvious to me that this particular clique was

socializing with competition as the root of everything. Maybe not *everything*, but it was certainly a prevalent factor. Trying to see who could get the better of others. Who could make the largest impact on the scene? Who was the loudest? Who had the best wardrobe? Which girl was the prettiest or had the most appealing figure? So much was based on charisma, whereas my friends were always more concerned with quantitative factors like grades. I intermingled pretty well and dapped up a few of the guys whom I was familiar with. There was a subgroup of kids from my class who I spoke with, but Zach was mainly familiarizing me with those from his group.

As I stated earlier, the most appealing thing about them was that they were a decently diverse group. There were Black kids who were perceived as being cool, all while appearing to be acting as their unapologetic self. Not really pandering at all. The environment was a candid microcosm of a diversifying suburb. It was akin to that scene from the movie *Clueless*, where Cher, Dionne, and Tai are walking through their school courtyard discussing the makeup of the student body and its respective cliques. Such an enthralling dynamic for someone who was still learning how to navigate within diversifying social circles. These were just my judgments at the moment. What I could gather from my vantage point, given what I had been exposed to up until then. It could have easily been inaccurate on many levels, as I wasn't personally familiar with most of the students. My perspectives at that time were solely based on optics and the little bits of conversation I was becoming privy to.

54

I witnessed Nicos mingling back and forth from person to person. He gave off the impression he was good friends with almost everybody out there. His voice projected well, and his mannerisms seemed a tad brazen, which isn't a negative critique in the least. Very comfortable in his own skin and confident about showing it. It was great to see an African American student behaving in this manner. In some ways, I sort of wished that I acted more like that.

I always had an affinity for aesthetics, so I noticed when a certain look stood out to me. On this afternoon, Nicos was wearing a denim Levi's jacket, baggy blue jeans, and light brown Timberland boots. The ones that would be referred to as the "butters" in urban slang. Years later, I would clown him for that fit, referring to it as a "Canadian tuxedo," but I secretly thought it was a pretty cool vibe. Very uptown New York City. Harlem-esque, like something that Roc-A-Fella Record's CEO, Damon Dash, would wear.

He would walk up to girls and casually put his arm around them while chatting. It toed the line between being overtly forward and lighthearted. One thing that it unquestionably embodied was outward confidence. This was contradictory to my demeanor, as my self-assurance was mostly internal.

Other than having a pretty smug attitude, my approach to interacting was fairly modest. Nicos came up and greeted me. He gave me props and said, "I see you've been ballin' out on that tennis court. Aren't you the next Arthur Ashe or some shit?" It was pretty funny. Nicos was actually built more like a tennis player than I was. He was about four inches taller and more narrow. I had more of a wrestler's build. Regardless, I knew I wasn't anywhere near as good as the late, great Ashe. Actually, many students would equate me to Ashe. He was probably the only Black male tennis player they were familiar with, so I suppose it seemed like an appropriate analogy. There was really no legitimate comparison between high school and professional tennis, but I couldn't expect the average person to be aware of that. I let the façade persist.

Nicos then asked me if Savannah and I had been seeing each other. I didn't confirm or deny anything. Just sort of brushed the question off as seeming frivolous. A very "whatever" type moment in terms of my response. He and I didn't say much else to one another on that day. It was a nice change of pace and I was able to make some new acquaintances. The bubble I had intently confined myself to was beginning to burst, but this was most certainly a necessary adjustment. It can be tough for us to make significant strides if we don't force ourselves into situations that cause us to question our welfare and our motives.

55

My relationship with Savannah was slowly starting to get awkward. It wasn't like anything was bad or contentious but just beginning to temper downward. I guess that's a common occurrence in relationships, which is something that I've become aware of as an adult but not so much as a high schooler who was new to dating. We still talked on a daily basis. She continued to visit me at my locker toward the end of each day. I'd drive her home from school from time to time. Movie nights at her house persisted, but the intimacy aspect of our relationship was the constant elephant in the room. Still no kissing and definitely no sexual activity. Despite all of the porn I had watched, I knew I wasn't ready. Maybe my exposure to adult content was causing anxiety in terms of engaging in the actual act. I really wanted to be ready, but I didn't feel it inside. So many other students were having sex on a regular basis, so I thought I *should* be ready, but when you're growing up, timing is such an important factor when it comes to momentous acts. If I forced something and it didn't go well, I could get completely embarrassed (it was the same feeling I had when I passed up on kissing her at the end of our first date). It would be social suicide, which was something I wasn't prepared to handle. Although I knew I wasn't gung ho about it all, the question of whether or not I would engage was still up in the air.

Savannah continued to name drop little aspects of sexual activity, sometimes referring to situations her friends were getting into. Other times being flirty to the point it seemed highly excessive, given the way in which we had been interacting. Despite her younger age, she was clearly sexually frustrated. Or maybe she was forcing the act just to get it over with. So many teenagers do it just to say they've done it. To get it out of the way. I couldn't be completely certain of her motives, but sexual frustration seemed to be the root cause of her actions. I mean, I had a lot of pent-up energy as well. I wanted to do it, but this didn't seem like the right time. These types of feelings manifest themselves differently in everyone.

I had a pretty impactful decision to make. The position I had initially wanted to be placed in was beginning to turn into a burden. How in the hell could dating a young wannabe sex kitten possibly turn problematic? Or would it not? It was occurrences like this that made me long for a parent I could lean on to discuss such issues. Someone to help dissect them while my sense of self was emerging. Their hands-off approach wasn't going to do me any favors with this particular conundrum. It was also then that I realized the isolation of the tennis court wasn't going to save me from everything. If our therapeutic needs aren't met while we are young, trauma can ensue. Confusion will always be prevalent as we grow, but an effective support system can help make sense of the bumps in the road. At any rate, you've got to push through these proverbial monsoons. Because our existence persists. Life can sometimes be all things wild, puzzling, and full of transcendent moments at the same time.

During the following week, Savannah's demeanor began to change. The school year was coming to an end, so that alone could prompt students to switch up a bit. Great weather, lots of sun, and more hours of daylight could be a massive mood lifter. Personally, I couldn't wait for the tennis season to conclude. The sport was beginning to become cumbersome. Slowly, I was realizing that playing for a Division I college wasn't in the cards for me, unless I tried to walk on, which was not a task I was willing to take on. There was no way I was going to be offered a scholarship. I knew I could easily play for a Division II or III school, but I had my sights set on Virginia Tech. For me, the summer meant a lot of hours on the practice court but less tournament competition. I'd have more relaxation time, as a significant break was needed.

Savannah seemed to be equally excited for the summer, but for reasons unlike myself. All she could talk about was how much time we'd be able to spend together. Dinners, parties, outdoor activities, etc. She was really attempting to push things forward and strengthen our connection. This was the first time since we started seeing one another that I'd seen her so giddy. We even started holding hands to and from each class. Up until this moment, the only times we held hands was when I'd walk with her to my car after school or when we'd relax on her couch.

These new actions were a tad off-putting, and I was clearly already becoming less interested. In all honesty, I was looking forward to spending my summer taking more time to myself. My alone time was becoming increasingly valuable to me. A disconnect was brewing, and it felt like a breakup was needed, although I suppose we weren't even technically together. Pretty laughable, I suppose. I wasn't willing to make that move, so I let the situation persist.

In addition to her attitude becoming more lovey-dovey, she began to dress in a more overtly sexy manner. Savannah was always pretty well-dressed. Nothing too outlandish, but in typical late '90s "preppy girl" fashion. Lots of American Eagle, Abercrombie, Express, and Gap. Trendy high school staples for certain demographics. Suddenly her clothing choices became far more fitted. Shirts that were cut super low to show off her cleavage. Low-rise jeans that would sometimes approach the crack of her ass. Skirts that were purposely too short in order to expose more leg and more upper thigh. I can't say I was complaining. I loved seeing girls dress like that. But this aesthetic choice was curious to me, and I was questioning her motives. Was this an attempt to get me revved up with hopes I'd be more inclined to have sex? Or maybe just a girl having fun with fashion while embracing her body? Regardless of the motive, I thought it was hot. If her goal was to arouse me, it was certainly working. Despite my heightened stimulation, I still didn't think I was ready for sex. Maybe things would change if I were actually put in a situation where I had to make an abrupt decision. The confusion continued to be all too real. Once again, this was the situation I had previously thought would be desirable. It was getting tough to cope with as tensions were rising. Tensions with respect to sexual activity and disconnecting relationship goals.

56

The weekend was approaching, which meant that one of us would attempt to schedule an evening together. I made the first move and asked if she wanted to go to dinner and a movie on Friday. Savannah appreciated the gesture but said she had plans with her older sister. They would have an early dinner at the local Applebee's before her sister had to be at work, so she wouldn't be home until around 8:00 p.m. She did invite me over afterward, though. That was totally fine, as it would give me a chance to go to the gym following tennis practice. `

The session went as planned. It always did. And my workout was typical. I did everything I would normally do. Got home from the gym at about 7:00 p.m., took a shower, got dressed, and completed my grooming routine (which always included a few spritzes of Obsession by Calvin Klein). It was about 8:15 p.m. when she called my house to let me know she was home from dinner. Everything was all good, and I left. On the way to her spot, I was bumpin' Beanie Sigel's *The Truth* album, which had been a mainstay in my car. I figured we'd just do what we always did. Maybe watch some MTV or HBO. *BET: Uncut* was usually entertaining after hours. There was bound to be a movie we would mutually enjoy. I knew that nobody else would be home, per usual, so we'd have complete privacy. My parents didn't set a curfew for me on this particular evening, so I could stay out until it seemed appropriate to leave. She told me the door would be open since she would be in the shower, and there wasn't anyone else around who could let me in. According to her, I could simply make myself at home.

I did just that, but to my surprise, the entire house was blacked out. Not a single light on. Usually, a popular sitcom would be playing on the television, but not tonight. I didn't hear the shower running, so I assumed she was getting dressed. The place sounded totally desolate. No rustling of any kind or doors opening and shutting. Not even the pitter-patter of footsteps. I had entered through the main level of their three-story town-home, which was common for me, so I expected to hear some activity—at least electronic noises of some sort.

I didn't turn any lights on, nor did I attempt to activate the TV. I was pretty fatigued after a long day, so I just kind of sat there and waited for her to come downstairs. It took her a while. Maybe fifteen minutes or so. The fact that the place was ill-lit wasn't helping because I was so drowsy. I almost completely passed out. Then, I finally heard a light, clunky sound approaching. It was soft but loud enough to awaken me from my dazed state. I raised my head and looked to my left, and there she was, dressed in high wedge heels and a robe. I couldn't tell what color the robe was, since it was so dark, but when she turned the kitchen light on, it was obvious it was a bold shade of crimson. Her lipstick appeared to match the robe perfectly, and the heavily tanned hue of her heels was equally coordinating. Savannah didn't say anything to me at all. I was silent as well. She walked over to me with that familiar giddy grin on her face and quickly straddled me. Like a jockey mounting a horse but with zero consideration for my torso.

There was no opportunity for me to do anything besides

engage or bail. I opted for the former. This was the pinnacle of my entire social existence. So many of my curiosities could be explored at this very moment. Upon positioning herself on top of me, she simultaneously started to kiss me while circling her hips across my lower body. This was one hell of a first kiss for us. Super zealous. I kissed back and used tongue, even though I was pretty clueless as to what I was doing. She took her robe off and exposed herself wearing a matching crimson-colored bra and panty set. We continued to make out in the same position while my hands gently dug into her back. Then, underneath her bra strap. This was by far the most erotic moment I had ever experienced. It was actually the only erotic moment I had experienced. Such a carnal bit of youthful vigor. I was like a sports car driver hitting top speed but having no idea what he was doing behind the wheel. Things were really heating up while she moved to kiss my neck and tightly gripped my shoulders. She forced my hands down toward her hips. I definitely did not resist. The jasmine scent she typically wore was stronger than usual, which I found appealing. Her lipstick was creamy and contained the aroma of lavender, which happens to be my absolute favorite. Our natural pheromones merged seamlessly. This happened so quickly and left me with a major decision to make.

My anxiety began to peak, and I thought about my readiness in terms of moving forward with the act. Clearly, the act that I'm referring to was full-blown sexual intercourse. Was I really ready to fuck? This was so difficult, because her kisses were really speaking to me. They said so much without any audible function. But what was more important was what my conscience was conveying. The devil and the angel were on my shoulders, sending mixed messages. Within just a few more minutes, it was evident the angel was winning. I knew it wouldn't be right for me to continue. I simply couldn't. Not without being untrue to myself. I had to force my way up. Leaving was imperative for my well-being. I wasn't ready for what was about to ensue. Whatever judgment or ridicule I received at school was just going to be something I would have to deal with. I gathered my thoughts, explained how sorry I was, kissed her one last time, and then left. She was saddened for sure. My actions could have made her feel inadequate. They most likely did. Regardless, I had to do what I had to do for myself. My drive home was filled partly with regret but mostly with solace.

57

Savannah and I didn't speak at all for the rest of the weekend. I had expected this would be the case. I didn't know how things would play out, but I was ready for whatever. I won't lie; apprehension was building for what I would be met with on Monday. This sort of shit comes with the territory. When you mix teenagers, sex, hormones, and emotions, a lethal concoction often arises. But I knew it would eventually be okay.

On Monday morning, Savannah didn't greet me at my locker as she usually would. She walked past me and simply said, "Hello." That was all, but I suppose it was a predictable course of action. She smiled, but it wasn't the same smirk I was used to. No spunk or perkiness. I was hurting because I felt I had let her down. I knew I wasn't what she had anticipated. I knew the relationship was over. Maybe it was really more of a "situationship" type thing? I guess it didn't matter. In high school, it was hard to decipher the nuances of our interactions. Especially those that warranted heightened levels of affection. I didn't know if we needed to talk things over or if it didn't need any explanation at all.

The day carried on, and my mind was doing its best Tron

impression like one of the bikes racing around the digital maze at supersonic speed. Sometimes flowing like water and other times wrecking repeatedly time and time again. No consistent motion. I decided to just approach her and apologize. Quick and easy. I didn't care if her friends were around. Simple closure was pertinent. At the end of the day, Savannah was gathering her belongings by her locker, and I walked right up to her. I asked her how she was doing and said I was sorry for what had happened. She assured me that she was doing fine. I asked if we were still a "thing." Her reaction was cavalier, to say the least. She shrugged her shoulders, tilted her head to the side, and walked away. That was cool, but it definitely created a cliffhanger. I rolled my eyes and walked away as well. Relationships can really be shitty at times.

The school year was winding down. Roughly two weeks left before summer vacation. It had been a few days since Savannah, and I had our little confrontation at her locker. It's strange how your mind can still be attached to a situation while you're doing everything in your power to set it free, especially as a teenager. This process becomes even harder when so many friends and acquaintances kept asking questions about everything. I still wasn't 100 percent sure about the finality of it, but I had to behave as if ties had been totally severed. Otherwise, I'd be hanging around acting like a complete chump, and I wasn't willing to play that role.

I carried on with life as usual. The end of the spring semester meant all sorts of banquets and awards gatherings, all of which were conducive to keeping me busy and my mind off of events that were fucking with my personal well-being. There was the Governor's School academic ceremony and the end-of-the-year varsity athletic function. Other less significant ones occurred as well. One of the more mundane events was the National Junior Honor Society conference. This was mainly a housekeeping thing. Discussing plans for the following year and having cupcakes, pizza, charcuterie, etc. It was a decent time, and it didn't require any travel, as it was held in the North Stafford High School library. One of the officeholders was reading the meeting minutes toward the end when my friend, Josh, barged in completely unannounced.

58

"Marlowe . . . Marlowe . . . did you hear what happened with Savannah?!" I was taken aback and surprised at what I thought was a very rude entrance. I had no idea what was going on. He followed up with, "Dude, I heard it was something with Nicos. I think they might have hooked up. Whatever it was, I heard that it was good." My mind was suddenly put into a tailspin, like a pilot going down without access to the control board. Josh's actions were bold and brash, but I really appreciated his candor. Had he approached it another way, I may have questioned our friendship. Beating around the bush just wouldn't have seemed right. I didn't know how to react as I was presented with such an unexpected piece of information. So, I responded in the most natural way I knew how.

I abruptly left the meeting. Not even giving the head of the organization any notice. I'm sure she knew that something had gone awry, but I'm not even 100 percent sure the event was mandatory. I frantically rushed to my car and headed straight to Savannah's house. Of course, I put my Beanie Sigel CD back in. Track one was called "The Truth." A Kanye West production before Kanye was really Kanye. Maybe it's ironic I was listening to a song with that particular title, given the nature of my situation. Let's just call it comfort music at this point. For whatever reason, hardcore hip-hop always puts me a bit more at ease. Even though the drive was only about ten minutes long, the level of tension I was experiencing subsided a bit as I got closer to her home.

I arrived and went right up and knocked on her door. She answered but seemed confused as to why I would show up unexpectedly. Savannah came outside and simply said, "So, what's up?" I looked at her like she was psychotic, and then she instantly realized why I had shown up. My face said it all. I was full of anger, irritation, and confusion, although each emotion was continuously lessening. Her response to my agitation was, "Well, look, we weren't together, so it's really whatever." And she was 100 percent correct. I absorbed the blow, even with my ego being bruised. I nodded my head and agreed with her, as much as it pained me to do so. I felt defeated, even though I really had no valid reason to.

Maybe my sexual uneasiness drove her to look for it elsewhere. I mean, I never even asked her to be my girlfriend, so what leg did I have to stand on in terms of voicing any amount of jealousy? Was I in the wrong here? Why would Nicos go and hook up with her? I know he and I weren't really close friends, but isn't some sort of bro code or decorum warranted? These questions ran through my mind while I stood there next to her. My contemplation didn't last long, as a vehicle sped down her street and then stopped on a dime right in front of her house. One of our mutual friends, Sean, got out of the passenger side and just looked up at Savannah with disgust. He had already heard what had happened through the grapevine and apparently found her actions to be immoral. Maybe he was sticking up for me. Or maybe he had a thing for Savannah and didn't want her messing with anyone at all. I really didn't know or care. He got back into the car and rode off to his house.

I don't think I said more than five sentences while I was on the porch with her. And after Sean sped away, I left soon afterward. My heart rate continued to decrease. I chilled out some more. I began to realize I didn't care nearly as much as I had initially thought. My issue was that another entity had infringed upon my perceived "comfort zone." The funny thing is that the comfort zone wasn't even totally comfortable. It was mostly about a possession being removed from my grasp. The state of affairs was complicated for me. This type of thing constantly happens to adult couples who are in committed relationships, let alone teenagers who don't know what in the hell is going on. At this point, my anger and confusion were null and void. I knew what had happened and why it had happened. Closure may have been desired, but it definitely wasn't necessary. Maybe a good night's sleep would help put it all at a distance.

Although I was in a fairly reasonable place mentally, something minuscule still wasn't sitting right within. I was maybe 80 percent complacent and 20 percent besieged. The whole notion of a possession being removed was gnawing away at me. I tossed and turned in bed, unable to find peace. My ego was compromised, and I wanted to try to get that possession back. In hindsight, I recognize that viewing human beings as possessions is an exceptionally flawed concept, but at seventeen, I just went with my gut. I didn't want her back because I actually cared. I didn't have a strong desire to be with Savannah. It wasn't like we had been close friends. There were no familial connections. I wasn't in love. Hell, I didn't even lust after her enough to have an intense desire to have sex.

At this point, I was basically playing a game and confronting a challenge. I was right at the cusp of beating *Super Mario Bros. 3*. It was level eight, and I was at the gates of Bowser's Castle. The catch was that I only had one life left. A single opportunity to rescue the princess from the embrace of the grotesque anthropomorphic turtle. One opportunity to seize the moment. The moment I really didn't even want. A complete paradox of motives and desires.

It was about 2:00 a.m. when I decided to get out of bed and head to our computer. It was in the basement, so I had to be especially quiet so that nobody was awakened. Once I arrived, I logged into our family's AOL account and then used my screen name to access my personal information. I checked my email, which contained nothing besides a few frivolous pieces of correspondence with friends. I had decided I was going to construct a love letter as an attempt to get her back into my good graces. Maybe some flowery—and obviously fabricated—language would do the trick and I'd get her back. Maybe I'd be able to wrap her into being in the same middle-of-the-road scenario we had been in just weeks prior. My actions didn't make any sense, but I persevered through the nonsense.

I opened up a Word document and just started writing from the heart. I suppose that means I was lying throughout the whole thing, because my heart was pretty barren. Nevertheless, I was trying. This was my mind as a young adult, having never been in a relationship. If I must say for myself, I did a great job coming up with an amazing facade of affection. I had seen enough cinematic portrayals of love stories, so I figured I could satisfactorily mimic them. My overall goal was to try and say the things that Jack from *Titanic* was thinking. I had to tell the truth, even in my lies. I don't think I even spell-checked the piece. I trusted my grammar to be solid, and once I was finished, I went ahead and sent it. Done. This was the point of no return.

My anxiety was fairly high in terms of waiting for her to respond. What if she actually wanted to get back together? Would that contribute to even more stress, seeing as though I wasn't actually very interested? What if she felt like my whole attempt was a joke and showed my email to all of her friends? Would I be ridiculed to no end? At this point it really didn't matter because the letter was sent. Relaxation was key for me at this juncture. I chilled out on the couch and watched the E!

channel. An episode of *The Howard Stern Show* was airing. At least I could get a good laugh in while I was wide awake. I didn't have to wait long for her reply. She got back to me within a few hours. Maybe she couldn't sleep either. Her email was short, to the point, and sincere.

59

Justin,

Thank you so much for your kind words. I really appreciate the gesture, but I think that this whole thing is over between us. It just isn't going to work. I wish you well. You're a great guy, but we aren't right for one another.

Kindly,
  Savannah

I guess it was really over, which was fine. It should have been. Her response provided closure for me, although my little last-ditch effort was completely fabricated and selfish. Very selfish. My ego was wounded, but not to the point where I was struggling any longer. During my last week at school, the questions from peers began to subside. Savannah and I continued to be cordial in the hallways, but that was the extent of our interaction. This was for the better. It was good we were still friendly but anything more intense could have been problematic. It was way too soon to behave as if nothing had been broken. Summer break couldn't come soon enough. I needed some relief from people. I was tired of putting on a front for a relationship I wasn't wholly invested in. Tennis was draining me and destroying my desire to compete. Still, I had about five more school days to endure. Five days until temporary freedom. A proverbial exodus from stressors.

Wednesday afternoon came around, and I approached the school exit hallway. Tennis was over, so I didn't have an urgent need to be anywhere. I could take my time mingling with friends or just linger around at my discretion. Any remaining anxiety I was feeling had pretty much dissipated, so my head was fairly clear. I sat alone at one of the cafeteria tables and rummaged through my book bag. Most likely looking for some nonexistent assignment just to kill time. I probably spent about five minutes sitting in silence, fumbling over a bunch of nothing. Just some generic papers and unnecessary folders.

Unexpectedly, Nicos came over and tapped me on the shoulder. This was the last face I had expected to see. He and I exchanged our hellos and dapped each other up. It was clear to me in that moment that he was going to be contrite about whatever it was he wanted to discuss. His demeanor was solemn, almost as if he was prepping to get something off of his chest. He was aware that I had heard about whatever had occurred between him and Savannah, so he cut right to the chase. Apparently the two of them had been hanging out on her porch and one thing led to another. He did tell me that they hooked up but didn't go into any specifics. I didn't ask either. In high school, "hooking up" has an enormously vague connotation. Had he divulged something that was a bit racy, my emotions might have been stirred back up into a tizzy.

He apologized for getting with her and even mentioned that the first thing he asked was whether or not she and I were still seeing each other. She had told him we weren't, so in his eyes, anything was fair game. I certainly couldn't fault him for that. I couldn't even fault her for the response she gave, as we weren't together at the time. Technically, we hadn't been "together" at all. I accepted the apology and we actually laughed about the situation soon afterward. I was slightly offended by the fact that he cared about apologizing. Maybe it was a bit of his compassionate side showing. Something he may have gotten from his mother and grandparents. Had the shoe been on the other foot, I don't know if I would have cared enough to say anything. I'd probably have just brushed it off as a general passing occurrence. Maybe . . . I don't really know, but I think that's how I would have handled things. Of course, in the back of my mind, I wondered what had actually gone on, but it wasn't the time or place for particulars. There was no reason to continue to hash out what had transpired between the two of them, so I went right into asking him about his musical tastes.

Weird segue, right? Like I said, I can be awkward at times, so I led with my comfort zone. He mentioned being a huge fan of the R&B group, Dru Hill. Their lead singer, Sisqo, had recently released a solo project, which I had purchased months prior. His single "Thong Song" was a major hit record we both thought was hella cheesy but loved its remix because it featured a rap verse from Foxy Brown. The track also contained minor differences in the production, which we both picked up on and found appealing. I often find the specificities of music to be intriguing to discuss, as was the case with him.

The dialogue was refreshing and different from conversing about music with others. Having a fruitful artistic discussion with another Black male felt comforting. The two of us were both students of the game, in terms of digging into the liner notes of albums. Recording projects are full of so many facets outside of just who sings on the songs, and it was clear we had a decent amount of knowledge about the producers and writers who worked with so many of the popular artists of the time. I followed up by asking who he thought was the greatest singer in music history. His GOAT, if you will. I get exceedingly judgmental about this type of question, and I'm completely okay with that. I don't care that my music snobbery can peak at times. It's part of my general makeup. When I get around those who I think know more about it than I do, I find it to be a very inviting trait, as I love to learn from others. With respect to my question, Nicos didn't hesitate before answering with, "Michael Jackson." Actually, he glared at me as if it would have been absurd to answer with anyone else. It was a comical moment, mainly because I concurred on all levels. There are an abundance of artists I think can contend for the title, but I've always been biased in favor of Michael. I guess Nicos felt the same.

My ensuing question was to address his feelings on George Michael. Not so much in terms of being the second best ever, but more as a general talking point. His eyes got wide, and he followed up by saying, "That's a badass White boy!" Honestly, it was such a perfect answer. That dude was an OG. In my opinion, analyzing a blue-eyed soul is always fascinating. I actually hate the phrase, but I use it because it's universally understood as referring to White people who sing R&B music. It was another little amusing slice of our conversation. Clearly, I agreed. Seeing if we felt the same was the entire point of me bringing him up in the first place. Ever since living overseas, George Michael has held a special place in my heart. His *Faith* album was really something special. Most would judge someone for mentioning an artist who was openly "out," but that wasn't the case here.

The moment was uplifting, especially considering everything that had transpired. Surprisingly, we ended up realizing we lived on opposite sides of the same small neighborhood. Easily within walking distance of one another. We talked for a few more minutes, but we both had places to be. Nicos was a really cool guy. I'd say he was a great guy, but I didn't know him well enough to make such a claim at the time. At that moment, the two of us became more than acquaintances. Not close, but definitely friendlier than before. A perfectly strange situation, I guess. Certainly far from the norm in terms of forging a friendship. Summer had finally arrived. Maybe he and I would hang out again in the near future. . . .

ACKNOWLEDGMENTS

While this has been all a part of the creation of my first book, I'm incredibly thankful for those who have aided in seeing it to fruition. Every minute bit of input that others have given has been integral to the process. In all honesty, it's been more than integral. It has been entirely essential, as without these humans, I wouldn't even be close to where I am at this given moment, in terms of having completed such a piece.

Jill Carlyle and the staff at Empowered Press have been absolutely amazing while working with me on this project. Never in my wildest dreams would I have thought that I would have been approached by such a team via social media and that a bounteous relationship would be forged. Their overall knowledge of the publishing game has educated me in ways that are unimaginable and truly priceless. I can't thank them enough for all that they've done.

My initial legal team at the Eden Law Firm was nothing but an unbreakable rock and source of initial guidance as I decided to embark on this process as a professional creator. Had it not been for a whimsical chance interaction, I would have never even considered making the move to work with a law firm to support any legal needs. Having a solid core of intellectual, and professional, cohorts has favorably served me as this body of work has been churning away bit by bit.

As I reference the members of this scholarly syndicate that has aided me with my content, I make a point to start with Khalfani King. When I began writing back in March of 2023, he was one of the first individuals that I was comfortable mentioning my professional desires and goals to. Being another African American male that had experienced some similarities in terms of our upbringing led me to trust that his candid feedback would be genuinely beneficial during this journey. That was precisely how things turned out, and I am thoroughly thankful for his involvement, critiques, and detailed opinions.

Secondly, my old buddy, Amber Sam Chee, was someone I sought advice from on a bit of a whim. The Commonwealth Governor's School seems like eons in the past, doesn't it? Not having spoken much in the past twenty years or so made me a bit apprehensive in terms of seeking some slight guidance, but I reached out anyway. She's always been someone whose intelligence I have greatly respected, even if being very different from that of my own. Her responses to my inquiries were not always carried out in the way that I would have expected, but that has been mostly beneficial. With a slightly unorthodox approach, she's helped me process some of my assertions with a far finer toothed comb than would have occurred initially. I thank her immensely for that. In addition, I think that she may have occasionally been reading some of my excerpts while working from home (and while on vacation), so I definitely cherish that level of commitment.

Mary Kenyon is a friend that I really only spoke to regarding my writing process toward the completion of my tasks. She ended up serving as one of my editors/beta readers, which helped provide me with some phenomenal supplementary feedback. Her brash general honesty caused me some anxiety upon asking for her opinions, but I felt that it was necessary with regards to gaining some obligatory insights. I value her approach to providing criticism and have found the tidbits that she leaves to be mostly endearing. Our discussions have provided me with an increased ability to dig into my core and pull from internal components that would have been otherwise unlikely. It's been both enjoyable, supportive, and eye opening.

Finally, the most vital contributing individual to the development of this novel has, as expected, come from Nicos Eaton. The overall premise of my coming-of-age memoir would not have been possible without his authentic, deliberate, and resolute input. He gave information and relished intimate accounts that may not have otherwise been shared at all. Even when I felt as though I may have been getting too personal with my inquiries, he shared his side of things with enough contriteness to walk a straight and narrow line. Truly conveying his perspective and not convoluting it with what others may have felt. His approach added to *his* personal validation and directly affected the manner in which *my* overall story was told. I am truly grateful for you and am proud to call you my best friend. Love you, brother. And I supremely value you all! Much respect.

Much Love To You All,
    Justin

ABOUT THE AUTHOR

Justin Marlowe holds a Bachelor's degree from Virginia Tech and has worked as a public school educator for 16 years. His diverse upbringing and background as a high school tennis athlete shaped his unique perspective. With a strong foundation in sociology, history, and race studies, Marlowe brings a keen insight to his writing. In addition to being a budding author, he is also involved in fashion and media, notably through podcasting.